IT AIN'T OVER YET!

Also by Dick Grannan

AN UNINTENDED JOURNEY

The Story of One Man's Struggle with Prostate Cancer
2009

It Ain't Over Yet!

Big Seas in a Small Boat

Dick Grannan

Order this book online at www.trafford.com
or email orders@trafford.com

Most Trafford titles are also available at major online book retailers.

Printed in the United States of America.

ISBN: 978-1-4269-3512-1 (sc)
ISBN: 978-1-4269-3513-8 (e-b)

Library of Congress Control Number: 2010909036

Our mission is to efficiently provide the world's finest, most comprehensive book publishing
service, enabling every author to experience success. To find out how to publish your book, your
way, and have it available worldwide, visit us online at www.trafford.com

Trafford rev. 07/28/2010

 www.trafford.com

North America & international
toll-free: 1 888 232 4444 (USA & Canada)
phone: 250 383 6864 ♦ fax: 812 355 4082

To all those recreational sailors who are willing to
go offshore and heed the call of
blue water sailing.

I salute you.

"GOOD WRITING…SUCCEEDS OR FAILS on the strength of its ability to engage you, to make you think, to give you a glimpse into someone else's head – even if in the end you conclude that someone else's head is not a place you'd like to be."

MALCOLM GLADWELL *WHAT THE Dog Saw*

Acknowledgements

MY WIFE MAUREEN

NITPICKERS PROOFREADING AND EDITING
TORONTO

Preface

CROSSING THE NORTH ATLANTIC Ocean in a small sailboat is no longer a news-grabbing event. Recent advances in navigation and communication equipment, not available a few short years ago, have greatly improved the sailor's chances of survival and success. Nevertheless, the North Atlantic Ocean is still an ocean with many different moods and often extreme challenges.

In 1996 three Lake Ontario sailors, Henk Borsboom, Peter Becker and the author, all from Toronto, Ontario, decided to accept the challenges of the North Atlantic Ocean on *RABASKA* (*big canoe*), a thirty-seven foot Alberg.

Why would I now spend the time to write about such a historical journey so many years later? The main reason of course, is that the adventure had a huge impact on our lives and the experience and lessons of that trip sit constantly on the edges of our memories, ready to come into focus whenever we are together. It ain't over yet!

However, it was so much more for me. While at sea I was forced to put from my mind the daily struggles with schedules, time responsibilities, reputation, self-image, and self-imposed obligations and focus totally on one simple task, that of survival. Strange as it may seem I can now see that all of the duties of living in society ultimately boil down to the one same thing—survival.

This is the story then of an accountant turned skipper, a property manager turned navigator, and a retired senior citizen turned cook and deckhand, working together as a team and taking our turn in conquering the North Atlantic Ocean. If nothing else, it rearranged our priorities and enabled us to become more in touch with our daily experiences. This alone made the trip well worth it. What follows is an account of my personal experience in the vast and open sea. Hope you enjoy it.

Chapter 1

How did i end up in a small sailboat in the North Atlantic Ocean in the midst of a vicious storm not knowing if I would live or die? Why did I not just take a plane and cross to the other side in a matter of hours? This question goes to the heart of the recreational sailor. Mariners, working the huge freighters that ply the ocean today, want to navigate their vessel to the next port as safely and as quickly as possible. I propose that the recreational sailor's goal, first and foremost, is the simple joy found in the act of sailing itself: harnessing the wind and feeling the boat's hull lean into the water as it slices its way through the waves, somehow frees the human spirit. That is not to say recreational sailors are not interested in getting somewhere at the same time. However, the emphasis is on the art and skill of sailing the boat.

I retired from sailboat racing years ago, but Maureen, my wife, tells me if another sailboat appears on the horizon, I immediately start trimming the sails. The prospect of crewing on a trans-Atlantic trip was the ultimate opportunity to indulge my obsession with sail.

I have always been seduced by the sea. The house I grew up in was situated on a large rocky hill. The land at the back of the house fell away quickly revealing the flats below and the busy Saint John Harbour in New Brunswick. In the kitchen at the back of the house my father built a breakfast nook which butted up against a large plate glass window. The vision through this window revealed a panoramic view of the commercial docks in the harbor below and a glimpse of the famous Bay of Fundy. From this kitchen window it was possible to watch the ocean freighters, as they were maneuvered in and out of the docks by small tugs. I ate my breakfast every morning perched on the same side of the breakfast table as it afforded me a birds-eye view of the activity in the harbor below.

One cold morning on November 24, 1944, when I was fifteen, I was watching two small tugs attempting to back a CP Steamship, the *BEAVERHILL*, the fourth of the Beaver cargo liners, out of its dock and into the open harbor. As winter approached, the world famous tides, together with the rushing water from the river, made the harbor a very dangerous place. But this was during the Second World War, and it was necessary to get the *BEAVERHILL* to sea to join the waiting convoy headed for Britain. The outgoing tide would facilitate her departure.

Suddenly, as I watched in horror, that massive ship, loaded high with military equipment and munitions, began to break free of the tugs. The small towboats were losing control of the ship to the mighty forces of the peaking tide and the powerful back eddies of the out-going river. The *BEAVERHILL* was drifting sideways toward Navy Island farther up in the harbor.

My mother knew of my attraction for the ocean because of the many books I had in my bedroom: The Bounty Trilogy including *Mutiny on the Bounty, Men Against the Sea* and *Pitcairn's Island*, and *The History of the American Navy*, that is, the old navy of sailing ships and the ironclads during the American Civil War. My bookshelf included stories about the Elizabethan pirates who harassed the Spanish treasure fleets in the Caribbean and the pirates who attacked the shipping along the shores of England. I even possessed books about the nature of the ocean itself such as *Under the Sea-Wind* by Rachel Carson. I was an avid reader of the two series: *Tugboat Annie* by Norman Reilly Raine and *Commodore Hornblower* by C.S. Forester in the *Saturday Evening Post*. I had read *Two Years Before the Mast* by Richard Henry Dana and of course, Joseph Conrad's stories. I turned and looked at my mother with a pleading smile. She quietly whispered in my ear, "You can stay home from school today if you want." A rare concession on her part I am sure.

As I slowly ate my breakfast the *BEAVERHILL* suddenly stopped drifting and I could see she lay broadside against the rugged shore of the small island. The tugs desperately tried to dislodge her, but the tremendous tide of the Bay of Fundy reversed itself and the water level began to drop rapidly as the tide receded. At the same time the increasing flow of the backwater from the emptying river was forcing the freighter further up on the rocks. Suddenly, the deck was a frenzy as crewmembers were doing everything they could to prevent the ship from being left high and dry on the reef. The tide, with its twenty-four foot tidal range in the harbor, finally left the great Beaver ship solidly aground. Once there, the only hope of freeing the ship would come twelve hours and twenty-five minutes later with the return of high tide—but it was not to be.

By noon the ship was wedged so tightly that I could see most of the ship's hull below the waterline. The water was going down but the ship was refusing to descend with it and remained stationary. Then to my horror I saw scramble nets being lowered down the sides of the vessel and men clamoring to safety. Suddenly a huge crack appeared down the middle of the ship. As the tide continued to recede, the crack opened wider and finally the ship fell apart like a twig being snapped in the hands of an angry man. When the tide was at its lowest the bow portion of the once proud ship angled down the seaweed-covered rocks toward the west side of the harbor, and the stern was sticking out into the river, slanted backwards toward the center of the city. The return of high tide was never going to set that ship free to sail the ocean again.

Later in the day as the tide began its return, like a cornucopia, goods of all sorts began floating out of the open hull and the harbor was soon awash with some of her cargo. The ship, like a huge elephant, lay broken and destroyed before my very eyes, its entrails spilling out into the open water. I remained at my window seat in the breakfast nook until darkness descended and I could no longer see the horrible disaster below.

SAINT JOHN, DURING THE mid 1800s was a large shipbuilding center, its most famous ship being the clipper ship *MARCO POLO* that became known as the fastest ship in the world. Of course New York sailors argue that the *SEA WITCH,* built in Smith and Dimon's East River Yard in New York in 1846 for the China trade route, and later the California gold rush, was the fastest sailing ship ever built. Unfortunately, she later burned and was wrecked twelve miles west of Havana. It is claimed the *SEA WITCH* established records that stand to this day.

Our house, with its lofty perch, was built by one of those ship owners in the late 1800s. This location was chosen long before the days of ship-to-shore radios. The house was situated so that the original owners could see their ships returning into the harbor from various ports around the world. When my family took possession I was six years old. The previous owners, descendents of the original Shives family, had died leaving the estate with much of its furnishing intact. Included were large paintings of ships and scenes of the seashore. As I grew older, I discovered the attic, where in one corner I found an assortment of many dust-covered wooden boxes. Searching through the crates I soon realized they were sea-chests that contained ships' logs. There were also cartons of bank manifests, and other records of various sorts related to the world shipping industry. Later this material was donated to the New Brunswick Museum in Saint John.

I would sit on one of those dusty boxes, close to the small window looking out over the harbor, and read the comments entered into the logs years before by ancient mariners crossing the North Atlantic Ocean. My imagination knew no bounds as I crossed the ocean in spirit with them, seated on my musty perch, a beautiful hand-written ship's log resting on my lap, dreaming of the sea and being part of its adventure myself some day.

But I never followed that dream. In high school, I settled for a small sailboat on the Saint John River and later in life a larger sailing vessel on Lake Ontario. Like so many others, I call myself a sailor. After a lifetime of reading about the sea, I know what others have endured in small boats in the middle of the ocean. But a lifetime of reading and sailing small boats, no matter how large the lake, does not fully fashion an inland sailor into an ocean explorer. I consider myself a recreational sailor, a seasonal sailor at the best. I have always made my living on the land, not on the sea that I once so ardently desired. But, as a recreational sailor I have experienced the boredom of passage-making as well as the fear that a fierce storm can instill, even in the bravest of hearts. I believed my childhood dream had been forsaken long ago.

Chapter 2

Eᴀʀʟʏ ɪɴ 1996 I was forced to come face to face with my long lost romance with the sea. Suddenly, as if out of nowhere, I was invited to join the crew of *RABASKA*. The owner wanted to sail his boat to Europe and he asked me to go with him as crew.

It was early in the evening when I received a phone call from Henk Borsboom, the owner and skipper. He began by telling me he was planning to leave in May and he talked about the repairs that were currently being done on the boat to prepare her for the long crossing.

Suddenly I could feel my heart flutter. Perhaps the boyhood dream was still buried deep inside. I found myself hoping he was building up to an invitation to join the crew, but at the same time, I was afraid that he might actually ask me just that! I remember reading Joseph Conrad's words, "He—man or people—who, putting his trust in the friendship of the sea, neglects the strength and cunning of his right hand, is a fool! As if it were too great, too mighty for common virtues, the ocean has no compassion, no faith, no law, no memory." He goes on to say, "*Odi et amo* (I hate and I love) may well be the confession of those who consciously or blindly have surrendered their existence to the fascination of the sea." ("Initiation", *The Mirror of the Sea*). Would we be such fools to blindly and consciously surrender our very lives to the mercy of such a merciless sea?

While I was listening to Henk on the phone my mind was racing. If he asked me what would I say? If I turned him down, was I rejecting a long lost boyhood dream? Would I lose face among my sailing buddies in the yacht club where we moored our boat, a 33' Gib'Sea called *SQUALL*? Certainly we had no plans to make such a trip in our boat as we considered it too small for such a challenge. Everyone knows ships are big and boats are small. Ships are meant to sail on the ocean, and boats, to sail inland in places like Lake Ontario, or along the coast. Every year there is a small fleet of pleasure craft from Toronto that venture down the coast of the United States to winter in Florida, Bermuda, or the islands of the Caribbean. As early as the ninth century, and perhaps even long before, sailors ventured out to sea in boats, and boats have been making sea voyages ever since. But a boat is not a ship and a lake is not a sea. I had to ask myself, was the idea of making a North Atlantic crossing a realistic dream, or was it just part of the lore and language of many recreational sailors?

TO BE HONEST I did not hear much of what was said on the phone that evening as my mind sped through these various thoughts. Suddenly I heard the skipper say, "We were wondering if you would be interested in joining us for the trip across the ocean this summer?" He probably told me who the *we* were, but I had been so distracted by my own thoughts that I did not remember. He had asked me the question I wanted to hear, yet at the same time dreaded. Since I was not in control of my immediate emotions and fears, I frantically searched for an excuse to put off an instant answer. My wife Maureen was not home at the time so she became my excuse for not saying yes or no. I told him I was honored that he respected my sailing skills enough to consider me for a crew position, but that I needed time to talk it over with my wife prior to making a final decision.

I knew in my own mind what Maureen would say. We had casually talked about such a trip for many years on those few times my boyhood dream tried to surface. "If you want to sail across the ocean, go ahead as long as I can fly to meet you on the other side." Therefore, I knew I could give an answer on the phone that evening without consultation with Maureen. At the same time, I realized that previous conversations with her, were at best, discussions in theory. This time the situation was not one of if, but "Will you join us this summer?" I did need to talk to her; I also recognized that I was using her as an excuse to give me time to get my own feelings in order.

I pondered the problem for two weeks before calling him back. During that time I did speak to Maureen and she restated her original position. I could sail anywhere provided she could join us at the other end.

Because I am retired, I had no reason to refuse the offer to join the crew. However, I was filled with all kinds of negative thoughts. What condition will the boat be in? Was it big enough to withstand the wave action of the North Atlantic Ocean? How long would such a journey take? I did not want to be separated from Maureen and our own boat for the whole summer. Would the crew be able to get along together? Fresh in my mind was the incident where another boat from a nearby sailing club had set out on a similar adventure and was forced to abandon the plan in New York because the crew was unable to work as a team. I did not want to be part of a similar experience. If I overcame my fears, and decided to join the crew, I wanted to see the adventure through to the end. It has been said often that the boat can make the trip successfully, but it is the crew that will have the problems.

But these were not my deeper concerns. During the intervening weeks, my mind would not let go of all the negative possibilities confronting such a journey. My real problem was, if the truth be told, I was afraid of what the North Atlantic might throw at us. The Bay of Fundy, where Saint John is situated, is considered one of the foggiest areas in the world. The only possible place it could be worse is off the Grand Banks of Newfoundland where many a fisherman lost his life in that cruel and foggy sea. I remembered the mournful sound of the foghorn on Partridge Island at the entrance to the Saint John Harbour. It reminded us each morning and evening that the fog was closing in. As kids we called it the B.O. horn, after the ad for Lifebuoy soap, the kind Ralphie (*A Christmas Story*) had to sit with in his mouth for using swear words. Beee…. Ohoo was also a reminder that danger was nearby. I thought about sailing out into the cold North Atlantic, surrounded by night and fog, and being cut down by a freighter! I have been told that most ocean going ships rely heavily on modern electronics when at sea and the chances of them taking evasive action is very remote or even impossible. Small boats must look out for themselves. Even if there was someone on the ship's deck at all times, it would be impossible for us on a small boat to survive the crash or even be found if we managed to stay afloat.

If I decided to go I thought it might be a good idea to buy some kind of detector, as I knew *RABASKA* did not have radar. I dreaded the thought of sailing in the shipping lanes outside of New York City, without any means of knowing what killer ships might be lurking in the dark and fog! I knew *RABASKA* did have a metal reflector that might show on a ship's radar screen, but there was nothing on *RABASKA* that would tell us there was a ship close by, except our eyes. At best, our boat would be a very small blip on their radar screen. Our only other mode of identification at night would be a few weak riding lights, those colored lights that identify a boat and indicate the direction it is heading. Besides, I thought those little lights were dependent on battery power, and without a lot of fuel, I had some concerns about their reliability as well. I thought even a solar panel, which *RABASKA* did not have, would be a good investment. If the engine failed so would the batteries. A solar panel would provide enough energy to keep the lights burning at night, provided we got enough sunshine. If I decided to sign-on, I knew I would be able to relax a lot more once we cleared the shipping lanes.

Today, most boats are equipped with the latest technologies like solar panels, internet connections, weather stations, radar and other goodies that *RABASKA* did not have. No doubt these technologies enhance the safety and comfort of today's sailors. But in the end, the challenge is still the boat and crew in harmony facing that unpredictable mass of ocean water.

Chapter 3

How I admired those ancient sailors who were willing to sail off the existing charts and into the unknown. They had no idea what lay ahead, nor did they know what was hidden beneath the sea. The flat earth theory was mostly destroyed as the astronomers, observing the sun, the moon and other heavenly bodies, concluded that the earth was also a sphere. They did not know, however, that all the seas of the world were one. They did not have the benefit of a compass, as it did not come into use until the early 1100s. Existing accounts were filled with tales of monsters living in the deep waters, of giant squid and serpents waiting to entwine their little ship, or huge creatures, like Puff the Magic Dragon, rising out of the sea to engulf them.

Anyone who has kept a lonely watch on a small sailboat in strange waters at night understands that even in these modern times it is not difficult to have similar primitive concerns. A few years ago I was helping deliver a thirty-foot Nonsuch through the Great Lakes from Toronto to Chicago. I was on deck alone during an early morning watch. The night was pitch black. The only things visible to my eyes were the compass light and the little running lights on the bow of the boat. It was as if nothing else existed. I felt like a small child who had been placed in a room alone, with the lights turned off and no points of reference, a sort of existential angst. Falling off the face of the earth seemed like a real possibility! I could see nothing in front of me. We were moving through space and time alone in the darkness, totally dependent on a small compass light to lead the way. I prayed our course was the correct one, and that our compass was properly set. If the earth and its water was indeed flat, then sailing into the blackness could become a fearful experience.

EARLY FISHING FLEETS SPAWNED different customs that endured for many years. Superstition, for example, led to the ceremonies surrounding burial at sea. The body was put into shrouds made from sailcloth and weights were added to make sure the body sank to Davy Jones' Locker (The Devil Jonah's Locker – Jonah 1:15). From there they could enter Fiddler's Green, the underwater heaven. No one dared leave a bucket on the deck for they just might kick the bucket and fall overboard. And Shellbacks (sailors who have crossed the equator; Polly Wogs are sailors who have not) did not sit on an overturned pail because they believed misfortune would follow. And on it goes. Primitive fears burn deep and the unknown can always contain a nasty surprise. Our world still has its share of superstitions. We sometimes joke about opening an umbrella in the house, walking under a ladder, or even being careful not to let a black cat cross our path. We still provide children and adults with the fantasy world of Harry Potter, the Twilight Saga Series or Avatar. Fantasies, superstitions and many religious beliefs are still very much a part of our lives. So we should not be too judgmental of the sailors who sailed off into the unknown with their contemporary values and beliefs.

On another occasion on Lake Huron, again during a shift on deck in the dead of night, my imagination tended to run wild. We were miles offshore crossing Big Bay. The wind was strong and yet, in spite of that, the fog was thick. To compound the situation, we were in the direct shipping lanes. With the rest of the crew soundly sleeping below, I realized how much they depended on my ability to steer the course and move them safely forward to our destination. I stared constantly at the compass light to be sure I was keeping the boat on course. But the tiny light made it difficult for my eyes to penetrate the night and the fog. When I looked out into the black swirling mist, and the flashing white caps around me, I imagined I saw the bow of a large freighter bearing down on us. I kept peering ahead, to each side, and over the stern of the boat. I feared that something was out there ready to do us sudden harm. My one scrap of consolation was that I was on deck and awake, not asleep below in a bunk, where it would be more difficult to escape. My greatest wish was that dawn would come soon to dispel the demons that surrounded me.

When the sun eventually came out, what a wonderful experience it was. I was able to see again! As the mists burned away, the visibility improved, the night demons were laid to rest and my mind was free to dwell on breakfast and the warm berth below. I never liked night watches and their memories were back to haunt me.

But these tales, both ancient and modern, were not the only thoughts that triggered my imagination. My concern was the very real danger of being cut down at sea by a huge freighter in the middle of the night. Although our fears today are caused by different circumstances, nonetheless, fear was the common bond I shared with my imaginary childhood sailor friends of the Great Age of Discovery.

Recalling these past experiences it became even more difficult to call the skipper and tell him I was ready to come aboard. In retrospect, those two weeks of decision-making were by far the most difficult period for me. The thoughts of monsters even found their way into my dreams!

Finally, I pulled myself together, phoned the skipper and agreed to join the crew for the trans-Atlantic journey. Once that decision was made, it brought me peace of mind. My distorted fantasies and memories instantly dissolved as if by magic. Suddenly, I was calm and ready to put my energy into preparing for the journey.

Chapter 4

With my mind at peace, I now was able to discuss the situation at length with Maureen. I did not like the idea of separation for such a long period of time. But when I informed her that I would not be able to talk to her on the vessel's radio, she was shocked. She did not realize that distance would soon put us out of reach.

While sailing on the Great Lakes it was, and is, possible to use the boat's radio to contact the Coast Guard, who in turn can patch you through via telephone. Even better, today we just use a cell phone! With no sideband radio, we knew we would not be able to reach the Coast Guard after a few days at sea. She asked me to look for some alternative. Surely, I thought, some sort of satellite communication would be possible.

I decided to call Bell Mobility to see if they could provide me with a wireless phone that would relay messages through the satellite system. I had to call a number of locations before I reached anyone who even understood what I required. I finally learned that a portable phone would cost me $2,500 to rent and another $50 a minute to use! Not only did that sound outrageous, but also halfway across the Atlantic, I would have to make arrangements with a provider on the European side of the ocean at approximately the same cost.

Obviously, this idea had to be grounded. But it did strike me as strange that I could hold a small battery-operated device, the hand-held GPS, while it gathered and processed information from about 24 different satellites. The only cost for this service was the cost of the GPS itself, about $300. At the time I thought that perhaps in the future there would be something more reasonable. I spoke to the skipper and suggested sharing the cost and installation of a Ham Radio. He was not interested but we also realized we did not have time to prepare and pass the amateur radio exams. Finally, we decided that we could contact any ocean freighter and ask them to relay a message home. In the meantime, Maureen and I agreed that each time we saw the moon we would exchange greetings. After all, it was the same moon that we would be sharing together even if we were hours apart. Although in retrospect there were very few occasions on the ocean when the moon was evident, I certainly turned my thoughts to Maureen even if the moon was only partially visible.

When friends heard I was planning to sail across the ocean they asked me why? I told them that I decided to join the crew of *RABASKA*, not only to fulfill an unacknowledged dream of my youth, but that I wanted to experience what my Irish ancestors had to endure when they decided to immigrate to Canada in the 1800s. After all, my dream had been lost for many years, but my curiosity about my ancestors had recently been aroused by a visit to an Irish grave site on Partridge Island at the mouth of the Saint John River. I fully realized that those brave people had no idea what lay ahead of them. Nor did they have the miracles of modern sailing gear and navigational equipment to ease the hardships and anxiety they would have experienced in the middle of the ocean. Their goal was simply to escape from extreme poverty at home, especially after the Act of Union in 1803, and the Potato Famine of 1845. Many chose Canada because passage was much cheaper than crossing to the United States. Unfortunately, many died at sea and never reached their destination. I have always been thankful for those who survived, providing me with the opportunity to grow up and live my life in Canada.

JOSHUA SLOCUM, THE MAN from Nova Scotia who was the first to sail single-handed around the world in 1895, did so in a 36'9" sloop. He re-rigged his boat of choice as a yawl for the voyage. *SPRAY*, the 100-year-old derelict oyster sloop that Joshua Slocum used to sail alone around the world, was historically considered the ultimate cruising boat. He managed to travel 45,000 miles, but it took him three years. We did not plan to take that long to cross the North Atlantic! However, if Slocum's 37-foot boat was that successful, our chances of making it across the Atlantic in a modern boat were rather good. Of course, he was on his own, but he did point out in his writings that though skill was important, what really counted the most at sea, was character. "As for aging, why, the dial of my life was turned back till my friends all said, 'Slocum is young again'." As the crew of *RABASKA*, we were to discover these two truths of skill or character for ourselves.

Henk Borsboom, our skipper, is an experienced blue water sailor and a founding member of Bluffers Park Yacht Club in Scarborough, Ontario. Born in Holland, he sailed in the North Sea before moving to Canada. His first boat on Lake Ontario was a thirty-foot steel hull vessel that he completed himself. I had cruised with Henk on a number of occasions, and I knew he was a competent sailor and a very handy man aboard a vessel.

Peter Becker, our navigator, was also a seasoned sailor. Born in Germany, he now sails extensively on Lake Ontario. He also has blue water experience having sailed to Bermuda and other points south as well as coastal cruising. He too is a member of our yacht club and owner of an Express 30. He has a broad knowledge of the safety requirements necessary for a long voyage. Most of all, Peter has a tremendous sense of humor, a must on a long and confined voyage across the ocean. He is able to find the comical in the most difficult situations.

Thus, with an experienced skipper and a solid navigator, the only thing missing for the trip was a cook. I became chief cook-and-bottle-washer as well as deck hand.

Because each of us own our own boat, we considered ourselves skippers. I could see this as a potential for conflict from the very beginning. Sailing on the ocean in a small boat requires teamwork, but it is not a democracy. My experience has taught me that there is only room for one skipper, especially when decisions must be made quickly and without prolonged discussion. Consequently, I resolved that I would not attempt to second-guess the skipper, or suggest that his decisions were inappropriate. Being the oldest member of the crew, I probably had the most sailing experience. But if harmony was to be preserved aboard our small vessel, I realized that my task would be to provide good and healthy meals, take my turn on watch, and not challenge the decisions of the skipper.

RABASKA, AN ALBERG 37, built by the Whitby Boat Works in Ontario, is sloop rigged. Given the skipper's origins, this rig was rather an appropriate type of vessel as it evolved from Europe and had a Dutch designation (sloëp).

RABASKA's lines, or the silhouette of the boat, are classic with a long counter or stern section reaching out over the water, a full keel and what is called a spoon bow. Even though the boat is considered 37 feet long, because of the counter and spoon bow, the actual waterline of the boat is 26½ feet. The beam, the widest part of the boat, is 10 feet 2 inches. This is considered a narrow boat by today's standards. The freeboard, or distance from the water to the deck rail, is very low. It gives the boat a graceful silhouette, but it limits the living space below and allows the sea to roll over the boat in high winds. The total living space available below decks is approximately 278 square feet. But much of this was taken up by a table, bench seats, navigation station, head, galley and quarter berth. It was in these limited quarters that the three of us had to learn to live and work in close harmony.

At the end of the 1995 sailing season, the boat was transported to a warehouse near the Don Valley Parkway in Toronto for a refit. The boat had been sailed to Bermuda by the skipper and Peter in 1993. At that time, they discovered seawater was finding its way into the cabin. Henk thought that the leaking water came in through the chain-plates, where the wire stays that support the mast are secured to the hull of the boat. He was also suspicious that some of the leakage was through the hull/deck joint. The two parts had been bolted together to form the complete vessel.

Because of the low freeboard and narrow beam, we knew it was a wet boat. We soon found out how true that was! Unlike a powerboat, a sailboat needs to beat into the wind and heel over in the water. This means one side of the boat is low in the water, often submerging the rail at the same time. The other side, the quarter from which the wind is blowing, although high out of the water, could still take aboard large waves, which then cascaded along the deck to escape over the stern. Thus, the potential for leaks existed on both the port and starboard side in rough seas. Because there was a small guard rail around the cockpit, the crew supposedly would be protected and remain relatively dry.

The winter repairs were intended to stop the cabin leakage along the rail. None of us wanted to cross the Atlantic in a boat that was not dry and warm.

I visited the location once or twice to see how the work was progressing and to help where I could. This gave me the opportunity to examine the boat and to familiarize myself with its construction and layout.

During this same period, the mast was examined and repairs made where necessary. Having a mast fall overboard, thousands of miles from shore, would be a catastrophe. Thirty-five gallons of diesel will not get you very far on the vast ocean.

Chapter 5

Many in-land sailors who venture out over the ocean choose a southern route. They often sail south to Bermuda, crossing the ocean from there, and then work their way up to the Canary Islands. This can, in theory, be calmer and warmer at the right time of the year. We agreed on a more northern course, one that would take us across to the Azores (38° 45' N, 27º W) along the 40th parallel north and from there directly across to Gibraltar. I must admit I did not know at that time that the wind patterns form a tremendous circle in the North Atlantic. Apparently, they are northeast and easterly winds in the Trades above the equator, and then southwesterly along the North American coast. Then you get the wild westerly winds that can give fair wind to Europe, if you're lucky. But even if I had known this, I could not have envisioned some of the storms we encountered along the way. As Clive Cussler wrote in one of his books, "Nothing is ordinary when it comes to the ocean." Looking for a shortcut, we figured we could save close to 400 nautical miles, even though it would mean the weather conditions would not be semitropical. We realized that this route must be made at the proper time of the year, not only to take advantage of the right wind conditions, but also to avoid the flat calms common between the Azores and Gibraltar. We hoped that this course would also shorten our time at sea.

Fortunately, we had a wealth of information to help us make our decision. Since 1842, sailors had begun to gather the records of hundreds of ships and to analyze the wind direction, the currents, the flow of the Gulf Stream and the force of the sea. Unlike the charts of lakes, the monthly ocean charts record the averages of all this information giving us an approximation of what to expect as we moved across the chart.

Our decision to sail the northern route then was not based on speed alone, but on the cumulative recorded experiences of those who had gone before us.

PETER WOULD PLOT OUR course each day on a large North Atlantic Ocean chart that Henk had purchased for the trip. We were all familiar with this type of navigation as we were sailing before the introduction and availability of GPS for small boats. This was definitely one advantage we had over ancient sailors.

Even ancient maps and charts came with some sort of grid system. Where to place the parallel lines of latitude was generally accepted, but it took hundreds of years to come to an agreement as to where to place the prime meridian of longitude. Columbus had to navigate without a universally accepted starting point for the meridians of longitude. It was more than a hundred years ago that the Greenwich meridian as 0° longitude became the norm. Of course, the French wanted Paris to be that point! So compared to ancient times, plotting on a chart of the North Atlantic was a relatively accurate method for knowing your position. We were also blessed with an on-board GPS (Magellan 5200DX) and a smaller hand-operated GPS (Magellan 500DLX). Our chance of getting lost was a minor concern.

Finally, Henk installed a self-steering device that would react to the wind and water. It was rather awkward as it was connected to the boat's steering wheel with nylon lines. The wind vane could steer the boat on a given course by itself. It required, however, adjustments during a directional change in the wind if we wanted to stay on course. Adjusting this Monitor was the responsibility of the person on watch. That meant the helmsperson did not have to sit at the wheel for the full watch, but could snuggle up under the dodger for protection and check the compass course now and again. The problem with this open arrangement of lines on the deck was the danger of getting your feet entangled. But that inconvenience was well worth it given the freedom it allowed the helmsman. In retrospect, it was a good choice, as a powered auto-helm would never be able to handle some of the huge seas we encountered and would have used up what little reserve we had in our batteries.

Chapter 6

OUR STUDY OF THE charts of the North Atlantic had convinced us that we had to leave New York Harbor no later than June 1. The window of opportunity for avoiding bad weather and even hurricane winds was between early June and mid-August.

Our plan was for Henk and me to sail across Lake Ontario to Oswego, N.Y. where we would dismast the boat and prepare to motor down the Erie Canal to the village of Castleton-on-Hudson. Peter planned to meet us in New York City the night before we set out on our 3,500-mile journey across the North Atlantic. We had been through this canal before and figured that a week should give us time enough to reach New York City by the June 1 deadline we had set for ourselves. Reports from the canal were not good. It was a very wet spring and the water level was high, forcing the authorities to shut down some of the locks. The last thing in the world we wanted to happen was to be trapped somewhere in the lock system. The canal authorities could not give us a date for reopening the closed locks. We were told to wait and they would let us know when all the locks were operational.

MAY 14 WAS A rather special day for me. Maureen informed me in the morning that two of her sisters were coming over after dinner for a Bon Voyage drink. Later in the day, when we had cleaned up the dinner things, Maureen asked me if I would mind changing my clothes. Blue jeans and a T-shirt that said *I'm Retired—This Is As Dressed Up As I Get* was not considered appropriate.

Two of her sisters, Norah and Helen, arrived about twenty minutes later and I offered them a drink. We had just sat down when the door bell started ringing. I did not have a clue as to what was happening. More and more people began arriving until we had more than thirty people in our apartment. Maureen was well prepared and snacks and drinks of all sorts appeared from nowhere. I don't know how she did it.

To my delight, Brian Shelly and his wife Pauline, sailing friends for many years, arrived providing me an opportunity to pick Brian's brain. Brian is the author of *Without Rival,* a book that is based on his sailing experience in the Great Lakes, the North Atlantic, the canals in Europe, the Caribbean, and the Mississippi. I had crewed on Brian's racing boat for many years and learned a great deal about boat handling, and the importance of patience and respect for fellow crewmembers.

Finally, late in the evening Henk, the skipper, and his wife, came through the door and presented me with a beautiful jacket with the inscription *RABASKA* in gold lettering across the back. He brought some bad news as well. The canal was still flooding so our chance of leaving on Sunday was unlikely. He was thinking we might have to ship the boat by truck to New York if we wanted to stick to our planned schedule.

Maureen seemed to be adjusting to my imminent departure. I was still apprehensive, and as I performed little chores around the house, like watering the plants, I was thinking that this could be the last time I would ever see them. I am usually an upbeat person and I knew Maureen had confidence in the crew and understood we would take every precaution to be safe. Our mutual concern was the delay in getting the boat into the water and not having an opportunity for a good shakedown cruise before heading out on the ocean. Nor would we have an opportunity to test to our satisfaction, the repairs made to the boat during the winter months. We had hoped to use the time motoring down the canal to assess the new motor and to make any adjustments that might be required. Peter had made it clear to Henk that unless everything was in working order, he would not join us in New York. I did not like that news for the simple reason it would mean longer watches at night and less crew to operate the boat. This was another real concern of mine as I was depending on Peter to be there. I realized many recreational sailors do cross the ocean alone. I am not one of them and never intend to join that elite group. I like company, and I like assistance with whatever I am doing. Indeed, I resolved that if Peter decided not to make the journey, then I also would withdraw as a crewmember. None of us wanted this to happen at the last minute.

We had witnessed similar situations in the past. So Henk and I had to be sure *RABASKA* was fit and ready to take on the challenge.

IF IT WAS NOT possible to go to New York via the Erie Canal, Henk would have to arrange to have the boat trucked from St. Catharines, Ontario. We would sail the boat across the lake from Toronto, giving us an opportunity to test some of the equipment and at the same time make any necessary repairs.

The trip on the truck, we were told, would take one day enabling us to meet our departure deadline of June 1 out of New York Harbor. This would give us more time for preparations in Castleton-on-Hudson, but at that point in time, the final decision had not been made. We were still waiting to hear from the Erie Canal dock masters.

THE NEXT DAY HENK and I moved our food supplies down to the boat at the club dock. We just piled everything up below so that I could properly store the provisions according to the computer chart I had prepared.

The following day I went down to the boat and got to work putting the stores away. The lighter goods were stored in the port V-berth and every item was clearly marked on my diagram. I wanted to get the heavier canned goods down low and in the center of the boat. I did succeed in doing this for the most part, but the rest of the cans I double packed in plastic bags, tagged again and put them in unused sail bags deep in the starboard locker in the stern of the boat.

Although *RABASKA* was equipped with refrigeration, we clearly could not use it. It depended on the daily running of the motor, something we could not do with our limited fuel supply. So we decided to use that space for storing the food items we would be using for a few days ahead. Everything was clearly labeled and stored in its own space. When I was done, you would never know that the boat was provisioned for seventy days, unless you looked closely at the boot top on the outside of the hull.

THE NEW YORK IN-LAND waterway is a vast network of lakes and canals that stretch across the northern part of the state. Our original planned trip was to take us from Oswego, east of Rochester, down the Oswego Canal to Oneida Lake. From there we would motor through the Erie

Canal to meet the Hudson River near Albany. In Albany, we would re-step the mast before proceeding down the river to New York City.

Not willing to accept the comments of the lock master near Oswego, I suggested Henk call the head office and get the information right from the top. However, they were not much help as they said they had no idea how much longer they would keep some of the locks closed. Finally, Henk had to make the decision about trucking the boat to New York from St. Catharines. The plan was to sail the boat over to St. Catharines, dismast, load the boat on a truck and have it delivered to a marina in Tarrytown, further down the river than Castleton-on-Hudson, and about 30 miles upriver from New York City. The decision was finally made to do just that and we were then in a position to reconfirm our departure date.

Chapter 7

Two days before we left Toronto, I had completed the storage of all supplies and moved most of my own personal gear aboard. I used a large ski bag and packed my survival suit, safety equipment, sea boots, warm weather clothes and wet gear separately. But the large bag took up too much space in the hanging locker and there was not enough room for Henk's or Peter's sea bags. I culled through my clothing, discarding some and repacking the rest into a smaller bag provided by Henk. It was a blue canvas bag, but it had the advantage of having a waterproof lining. Nevertheless, I still packed most items in separate garbage bags to keep them dry.

Both Maureen and I were relieved that a departure date had been finally set and that it was decided that Henk and I would be sailing the boat to St. Catharines the following Monday.

Bright and early on Monday morning Maureen drove me to the yacht club. She had booked off work that day to see us away. One club member who berthed his boat next to ours was on the dock to bid us farewell, and Henk's daughter, who had driven him to the boat, remained as well. The five of us sat at a picnic table in the parking lot and shared some Tim Hortons coffee and donuts, trying to avoid the last good-bye. Finally, Maureen was the only one remaining and after an emotional separation, she helped us off the dock. We were finally on our way!

We motored out of the harbor as there was not a breath of wind on Lake Ontario that morning. I could see Maureen running back up the dock and heading for the clubhouse veranda for one last wave. I am not sure she could see me as we motored toward the horizon, but she was quite visible in a bright red blazer. I found the experience difficult even though I kept my feelings hidden from Henk, but I was thinking to myself, "Why was I doing this anyway? When, if ever, would I see her again?"

Our trip across the lake was uneventful and with no wind, we had to motor all of the way depriving us of an opportunity to test the sailing gear. We arrived at St. Catharines Marina at noon. Because the transport truck was due early the next morning, we immediately moved the boat to the dock with the mast crane. When we saw the small crane, we realized we should have removed the mast back at the club. We were forced to motor across the lake anyway, and the crane at the marina hardly looked capable of handling a mast as large as ours. To get close to the crane we had to go bow-to-bow with a beautiful 70-foot motor-cruiser that was being readied for delivery to the new owner. Being close to such a large vessel, *RABASKA* seemed small and low on the water by comparison.

As soon as the boat was secure, we began to remove the sails and rigging. It became apparent that we needed help with the hand-operated crane. It was very shaky and there was a danger that if the mast was too heavy, it would fall on the shiny new powerboat up against our bow. I went to the marina office and two men from the yard were dispatched to give us a hand.

By the time we had readied the boat for transport, it was late in the evening. We had skipped lunch as we wanted to have both the spar and the boat ready for the early morning pickup. We donned our newly minted blue and gold *RABASKA* jackets and walked into town for dinner at a small Italian restaurant.

St. Catharines is known as the Garden City as it has more than a thousand groomed parks, gardens and trails. But more importantly, the Welland Canal, a ship canal, runs 27 miles right through the city. On our way back from dinner, we were held up at a bridge that crossed over the canal. A large ocean freighter was slowly working its way down the west wall of the canal and was approaching the lock adjacent to the bridge. It appeared as if it were using the canal wall as a rub rail to keep it lined up with the entrance to the lock.

Finally, it began to move in front of us as we stood about three feet from the lock wall. Once again, as I peered up the side of this huge mountain of rusty steel, a chill went up my spine. Suddenly, yet again,

I was confronted by my fear of being cut down on the ocean. If we hit one of these huge ocean freighters moving at top speed in the North Atlantic, no one would ever know what happened to us. Even at its slowest speed, its might and power were self-evident. When it finally eased into the lock, with only inches to spare, the huge propellers went into reverse driving a surging wave along the walls of the lock. When the ship was finally stopped in the lock, the bridge opened and we made our way back to the boat deep in thought.

The weather dawned clear and warm the next day. Henk and I were up early to move the boat over to the launching area. A huge flatbed truck from Andrews Trucking was due at 1000, and we had a number of small chores to do before lifting the boat out of the water and loading it on the truck.

AT 1000 SHARP THE crew from the marina moved the hydraulic lift to the dock, lowered its huge straps into the water, and Henk and I maneuvered the boat into position. Once we were sure the straps were not pulling on any vital parts such as the propeller or rudder, the boat was hoisted into the air and moved into the parking lot. Steve, the truck driver, arrived 15 minutes later and backed the flatbed under the boat.

I have witnessed boats being loaded onto flatbeds in the past. It usually takes a few hours to get everything in place but this man really knew his job for he had *RABASKA* sitting level, properly supported and strapped into place, with all loose equipment, including the mast secured, in forty-five minutes.

The truck cab had only two seats so I climbed into the berth behind the driver. I could not see much, but it was very comfortable and I even managed to doze off for a few minutes. Henk sat in the passenger seat and we headed for the American border.

Because we were being transported through the United States to the Atlantic Ocean, we had no problem at the border and in no time, we were on our way to Tarrytown, N.Y. I traded places with Henk for a while, so that I could catch some scenery along the way. As we passed near the canal, I noticed tied up to one lock a number of sailboats with their masts lying flat on their decks. Obviously, they had started up the canal, or perhaps down the canal, although I suspect most of them were returning after a winter in Florida, but were now trapped by the high water. I was glad Henk made the decision to truck the boat, even though I was looking forward to the beautiful passage through the canal.

Late in the afternoon, Steve announced that we would be stopping at a good restaurant a few miles outside of Tarrytown. True to his word, we pulled into a McDonald's. I don't think Steve had a part-time job doing restaurant reviews! After dinner, we were on the road again and arrived in Tarrytown, New York around 2230. The gate to the marina was open so we just pulled into the parking lot and parked the rig for the night. Henk and I climbed up on the boat, found some cold beer and invited Steve to join us before he retired to the truck's bunk. It was a strange feeling, sitting high up over the other boats and watching the traffic on one of the bridges over the Hudson River.

Tarrytown is a village located on the eastern bank of the Hudson River about 30 miles from midtown Manhattan. I read somewhere that in 1780 during the Revolutionary War, a Major John André was arrested as a spy. He apparently was a British army officer who was on his way south but was stopped by three militiamen. Unfortunately, they found some papers stuffed in his boots, and based on that evidence they hanged him. I figured he was from Lower Canada and probably not the first Canadian to die during that conflict. Neither Henk nor I had any hidden papers tucked in our boat shoes!

ALL THREE OF US were up again at 0700 and the manager of the marina, a very pleasant and helpful man by the name of Ted, directed us to move the truck closer to their travel lift. In a matter of a few minutes, *RABASKA* was once again afloat but now in the waters of the Hudson River.

Henk and I immediately began to rig the mast. The rig on a sailboat can be compared to an engine's drive shaft, as it is the means of converting power (wind) into motion. The rigging consists of two spars, the mast and the boom, the standing rigging or all of the stationary wires that hold the mast in place, and the running rigging, or the various lines that control the sails. It took us more than three hours to get it back into shape and to check and double check, not only the rigging itself, but the lights and radio antenna as well. When we were ready to re-step the mast, Ted and his crew helped us carry it to the travel lift, which was equipped with an excellent mast crane, and we soon had the mast lowered through the deck and into its step inside the boat.

Unfortunately, when the boat was being repaired during the winter, the glass work around the mast stepping location in the deck, where the mast fits through into its base below, had been finished with a round, smooth rim. To keep water from entering the cabin through this opening there is a canvas collar that attached to the mast and the deck of the boat. We realized that the collar would clamp tightly to the mast, but would not fit on the round rim of the deck. We borrowed a power stone from Ted and ground the rim flat. The collar was then fitted into place and clamped to cover the wooden pegs and rubber doorstoppers that were to hold the mast secure and in place. Unfortunately, we did not get this installation correct, for once at sea, these pegs had the habit of falling out in rough weather allowing the mast to create ungodly screeches and groans as it rubbed up against the rim collar.

Our next job was to tune the standing rigging as much as we could before taking the boat out for a test run. It is really important not to have too much weather helm, or the boat will want to head up into the wind and slow down, making it difficult for the helmsman. On the other hand, too much lee helm causes the boat to fall off and head downwind. Finding the proper balance was most important, especially on a long voyage. So the idea was to adjust the wire stays carefully so that the mast was positioned in such a way as to balance the sail's pressures. At this time, we discovered that when Henk had the wire stays replaced, the backstay on the starboard side was a few inches shorter than the one on the port side. Getting equal tension took up a good bit of our time.

While we were affixing, or bending on the sails, a handful of retired sea captains were watching every move and whispering comments to each other. Dressed in my jeans, and, dangling my rigging knife at my side, I made every effort to appear most competent. When finished, we moved the boat away from the spectators and into our assigned dock #14.

THERE HAPPENED TO BE a café at the marina, but it was closed and new potential operators were bidding on the contract. We had to walk down the road about a quarter of a mile to the next marina, where we had dinner in Windows Restaurant. We had a great salmon dinner and watched the sun set over the Hudson River through the large window next to our table.

27

Although the night was cold, the next day proved to be a wonderful sunny day. As usual, we were up early, as we wanted to complete the provisioning of the boat. There was a supermarket nearby where we were able to purchase fresh fruit, potatoes, carrots, onions, garlic and bread. We also purchased four dozen eggs and had some steaks, pork and chicken put into their freezer to be picked up prior to our departure. Finally, we bought some Russian black bread, a kind of very dark coarse rye bread that, as it turned out, had a terrific survival quality and lasted us for many weeks at sea. I was still wrestling with the problem of storage for fresh goods. I wanted a cool place out of the sun, but with plenty of fresh air. We decided to buy some solid plastic laundry baskets and use them for that purpose. I wanted to avoid the mesh hammock-type slings that are popular with boaters on the lake. Although they allow for the flow of air, the constant swinging causes the string to eat into the outside of the fruit and destroy it.

When we got back to the boat, I rinsed the carrots and potatoes in water laced with a few drops of Javex, dried them carefully with a paper towel, and allowed them to sun dry on the deck before confining them to their laundry basket home. Unfortunately, they were not as fresh as I would like, as Tarrytown is far from being a farming community. I left the eggs in their cartons, but I carefully wiped each egg with Vaseline to block out the air. These were then carefully stored high on the starboard side where I could get at them easily for frequent turning. Again, it would have been better to get farm fresh eggs that were not refrigerated, but that was out of the question.

We spent the rest of the day scrubbing the road bugs off the boat. Thousands of them managed to come aboard on our truck trip down the highway.

That evening I treated Henk to dinner at a small family restaurant on Main Street. After dinner, we walked around to take in the sights of Tarrytown. Tarrytown is a commuter town and because it is located on the river and the train lines, the cost of homes is astronomical by my standards. Only residents are allowed to park in town and there are severe fines and towing fees for anyone from the outside who would dare to park, even in the lot belonging to the supermarket. Parking a vehicle, of course, was not one of our problems.

On the way back to the boat the sun was setting over the river and the temperature was dropping rapidly. I stopped at a public phone and called Maureen in Toronto. She had some good news and some bad news. The good news was that I had won a 21-foot Hobie Cat in a charity lottery. The bad news was I had to take the boat and could not opt for a cash substitute. Maureen asked me what I thought the boat was worth and I said about $3,000. Much to my surprise, she said it was listed at $16,500! Not a bad return on a $100 ticket. But what was I to do with the boat? We already had *SQUALL* back in Toronto. I suggested that we strike a deal with the supplier. I figured that if I could get about $10,000, it would definitely be a good deal, for the supplier and for me. When I got home that is exactly what happened.

When I returned to the boat I told Henk about my good fortune, and then turned into the port berth for the night. Henk had been sleeping forward in the V-berth, but knew he would have to move once we got to sea. He had already decided he would shift to the quarter berth. So that left the starboard berth for Peter. It did seem that Henk and I were staking out our turf even before Peter arrived! However, since only the port berth was equipped with a lee cloth, or bunk guard that prevents the crew from falling out in heavy weather, the floor turned out to be one of Peter's favorite spots.

FRIDAY, MAY 31 WAS to be our last full day in port. Henk was having trouble with the handheld Magellan GPS. For some reason it would contact the satellites, but it would not do the calculations. Ted told us to talk to Jack, the owner of the motor launch *EARLY SPRING*. Jack looked at the Magellan and decided it had to go back to the factory for repairs. Peter had made it very clear that we had to have two GPS computers on-board for verification and back-up.

Jack told us he was going to the city later as he needed some things from a wholesale marina there, and he would be happy to take us along if we wanted to go. We agreed, and we were off to Long Island Sound to visit one of the largest boat supply stores I have seen. Henk immediately went to the GPS counter and asked for the cheapest GPS they had in stock. They produced a Magellan 2000 for less than $200 U.S., and Henk bought it as our back-up computer. I told Henk that when we returned to Canada I would buy it from him for our own boat on Lake Ontario. I have it and it is still working to this day. Now at least we could inform Peter that we had the required back-up equipment. I did not want Peter to back out at this late date.

I also took the opportunity to discuss my idea of a radar detector with Jack. He had worked with the U.S. government in the development of radar during the Second World War. He made it very clear to me that my idea would not work, if for no other reason than that a few hundred yards warning would not be enough. He also suggested that the Sea Radar Detectors, available in boat supplies stores and retailing for about $500 U.S. at that time, would also be a waste of money.

As Jack was so kind to drive us to the store, we invited him to lunch. He chose a small, but very friendly place, where we had an excellent lunch. During the meal, Jack told us the following story:

A number of years ago Jack, his wife and two small children set out from New York on a forty-foot sloop. They were only at sea a couple of days when they encountered winds that reached over seventy miles per hour. The wave heights were over thirty-five feet. Unfortunately, this condition persisted for nine days and nights. Everyone on-board was seasick. Even with all of the sails down, the boat was surfing down the sides of the waves at hull speed, as fast as it could go. The whole family lay on the floor of the cabin unable even to clean up their own sickness. It was so bad, Jack told us that he and his wife seriously considered opening the seacocks and sinking the boat. They felt they could no longer endure the horrible and terrifying conditions. What prevented them from following that course was the presence of their children. If the children had not been aboard, they felt they would have ended everything, rather than continue to endure those awful conditions.

Like most storms, it finally abated, and some time later they managed to limp into the Azores. When they returned to New York, he sold the sailboat and bought the powerboat, where he and his wife now live year round.

He was a very helpful man, but I did not need to hear that story, on that particular day, and I prayed his story would not be repeated on our trip.

We managed to get back to the boat by mid-afternoon. We immediately moved to the fuel dock to top-up the diesel and fill our water tanks so that we would be ready in the morning. Then we motored out into the river to complete our tuning of the rigging. Unfortunately, there was little wind so we tuned as best we could, checked all the running rigging to see that it was working properly, and made sure there was nothing on deck that was not secured. Back at the dock, we put the cotter pins into the turnbuckles and then taped the pins so that they would not rip the sail or come loose later.

There was a sharp turn in the weather during the afternoon. It turned from very cold to hot in a few hours. The locals said that the warm weather was more normal for that time of year. We were sitting on the deck enjoying the sun and waiting for Peter to arrive from the airport. The tide tables made it clear that we could not leave till the incoming tide turned. The current running upriver would double our time getting down to New York City. We decided to wait for the outgoing tide which, according to the tide chart, would begin shortly after noon the next day.

Peter arrived toward evening and his reward was to take us to dinner at Windows. Because of the warm weather, we were able to sit outside by the river, and again enjoy the setting sun. We were obviously excited as we chatted about our adventure. On our return to the boat, Peter decided that he was going to sleep in the starboard bunk. During our short stay in Tarrytown, I was able to get myself into the mood that this was simply preparation for just another cruise. But as I rolled into my sleeping bag that last night at dock, I was beginning to feel the tension once again.

Chapter 8

JUNE 1 HAD FINALLY arrived. In the old days of sailing ships, a voyage was never from one place to another. For example, the sailors would not say they would be sailing from New York to Gibraltar. Rather they would say they'd be sailing *toward* Gibraltar. The ultimate goal is to get to Gibraltar, but the sea, the wind and the waves present a certain element of uncertainty, hence the use of toward rather than *to*. Since we were about to begin a trip of more than three thousand miles, or approximately 5,000 km, in a small sailboat across the North Atlantic Ocean, saying *toward* Gibraltar seemed to make more sense even if the use of that word carried certain overtones. But I had already spent enough time mulling that over in my mind!

We awoke full of expectations. I walked down the dock to make some phone calls. I first called my sister in Montreal to say good-bye to her. If anything was to happen, she was to be the contact for my family back east. I know she thought I was rather foolish in making this trip and I wanted to reassure her that everything was going to be all right. I was full of emotion when I finally hung up the phone. When I made my next call to Maureen in Toronto, I had to try twice as hard to make it sound as if I was just off on another cruise.

Maureen now understood that we would not be able to communicate by radio. We again reconfirmed our commitment to make the moon our constant point of contact. When she looked at the moon, she would remind me of her love. I would do the same thing during a late watch, as I looked up into the magnificent night sky. At least that was the plan. Although this was a simple plan, the reality was we did not know then that a massive low-pressure system would obliterate the moon over the ocean for most of our journey.

The hurricane season that summer officially began on June 1, the very day we set out, and ended in late November. There were thirteen major storms, nine of which attained hurricane status and six became major hurricanes. In late June, hurricane Arthur started things off. It was followed by a really bad storm called Bertha in early July. These storms usually blow themselves out over land or when they move over cold water and wind shears. Since hurricanes tend to track north, Arthur's remains headed in our direction. A National Hurricane Center Report stated, "The remnant of Arthur was tracked for another thirty-six hours and was last identified about midway between Newfoundland and the Azores where it was absorbed by a much larger extra tropical low over the North Atlantic." Arthur's remnant had no trouble that summer locating *RABASKA* and her crew of three!

THE LAST CONVERSATION THAT day with Maureen was extremely emotional for me. I knew I might be exaggerating the danger, but I still harbored the thought that an accident could occur, or Mother Nature might have other plans for us. So it was very painful to say good-bye to her as I thought of the possibility that this could be our last and final exchange of love. On her part, she never let on that she was deeply worried, and it was not till my arrival back in Toronto that I learned about her apprehensions. I cried all the way back to the boat and had to pause along the way to wipe my eyes and compose myself before rejoining the crew on *RABASKA*.

At 1115, we cast off the lines that bound us to North America, left Dock #14 behind and moved out into the historical Hudson River. The incoming tide was approaching slack as we turned the bow downriver. By the time we reached the nearby bridge, the current and motor were carrying us toward the vast North Atlantic Ocean. Our intention was not to put up the sails until we cleared the harbor entrance thirty miles downstream. We wanted to give the boat's batteries one last charge and hoped to reach the ocean before nightfall.

Although I had sailed up and down this river before, this downriver cruise seemed different. The sense that I would be returning this way in a few weeks time, as Maureen and I had done on our own boat in the past, was missing.

When we reached the East River, we entered into Upper New York Bay, New Jersey on our starboard and Brooklyn on the port side.

The wind picked up as we moved down the river. Battery Park and Governors Island, both forts visible from the deck of *RABASKA*, were built in the 19th century to guard the East River entrance.

It was the great Greek philosopher, Aristotle, who once wrote, "The city is the teacher of man." We could see here and there what seemed to be abandoned waterfronts and their derelict piers as we slowly glided past the New York shoreline. I envisioned this great harbor in the 1800s full of sloops, schooners, brigs and other ships carrying passengers and cargo from around the world. Signal flags announced their arrival or departure as they jockeyed for space in the harbor, and goods from all over the globe would have been unloaded and piled on the docks.

Today New York and New Jersey are still bustling seaports moving millions of tons of cargo, but now in huge container ships, tankers and bulk carriers. No longer are there hundreds of workers, businessmen and citizens swarming the docks, but huge terminals and tall glass towers that in a sense hide the colorful activities of the past.

Of course, that day standing above it all were the twin towers of the World Trade Center, its foundations begun in 1967 and still soaring one hundred and ten floors into the air. It, more than anything else in the harbor, symbolized the history and importance of this great port city. We did not suspect then that its terrible destruction on September 11, 2001, would spread fear around the world and that Canada and Canadians would be drawn into what has become the longest war in the West in more than two hundred years.

As we motored along, our Canadian flag fluttering merrily on our stern, the Americans did not take alarm, for we passed their old forts quickly heading to the open water. The outgoing tide in the harbor, rushing against the incoming wind and waves, provided us with a bumpy ride through the murky waters of the river.

One other great symbol along the way was the Statue of Liberty located on what is now called Liberty Island. At one time, it was known as Bedloe's Island and was the home of Fort Wood, nicknamed Star Fort because of the shape of its fortifications. It is interesting to note, symbolizing once again the history of this great port, that the Chinese students carried replicas of that statue during their demonstrations in Beijing's Tiananmen Square.

There were a number of large ships and barges anchored as we motored through the harbor. Some huge container ships were taking advantage of the outgoing tide, and leaving the harbor for the ocean as were we. One box boat moved very close to our starboard side, its containers piled high, resembling a moving apartment building or a row of townhouse condominiums. I wondered if they could see where they were going, as the intermodal containers seemed to block the view from the wheelhouse. Originally, the first container ships were converted tankers left over after World War II, but today these modern polluters transport almost 90% of non-bulk dry cargo around the world.

Chapter 9

At 1530, we passed under the Verrazano Narrows Bridge that connects Brooklyn and Staten Island. In 1524, Giovanni da Verrazano was sailing up the coast and while looking across the Outer Banks of North Carolina, declared that he had found the Pacific Ocean. Little did he know that more than 3,000 miles of landmass stood between him and the Pacific. He is considered the first European navigator to enter New York Harbor and the Hudson River, hence the name of the bridge.

Coney Island, its beaches filled with Saturday sunbathers, was on our port side and Sandy Hook Bay opened up as we entered Lower New York Bay and motored through the Ambrose Channel.

One hour later the Verrazano Narrows Bridge began to disappear into the smog and I suddenly realized that we were leaving the land behind and were now on our own at sea. For a moment, I felt isolated and alone, but the skipper ordered the sails set and this sudden activity on deck, after a long day of sight seeing, was a welcome relief. The motor was shut down and the only sound became the wind and waves as the boat leaned into the salt water with all sails set. As the wind began to pick up, we were forced to reef, or shorten, the mainsail. We were off and running, underway at last with a bone in our teeth.

Prior to the trip, we had discussed who was going to do the deck work. Even though each of us was tethered at all times, or at least that was to be our unbroken rule, working on a pitching deck, especially in the dark, is dangerous. Before leaving the dock we had strung Jacklines along the deck on each side of the boat. Since we were going to be at sea for an extended period, they would remain there until we reached our destination. Our lines were made of high strength nylon webbing which will not roll under moving feet. They were secured to a pad eye at the bow and stern of the boat. Every time one of the crew came on deck, they were to attach their tether to one of these lines. In retrospect, I made one mistake in my choice of a tether. My tie, which was six feet long, had a snap shackle at each end. One end attached to the D-ring on the built-in harness on my survival suit, and the other snap shackle attached to the Jackline. A better arrangement would have been to have a quick release shackle on my vest so that if the boat went over I would be able to release the line and escape.

Another problem with this arrangement was the tether could, and did, arrest movement on the deck if it snared on a deck fitting. Because of the various obstructions, it was necessary now and again to unhook it in order to get past an object, thus exposing oneself to a sudden lurch of the boat.

For some reason it was agreed that Henk would do the majority of the foredeck work. After all he was not only the owner and skipper, but also the youngest member of the crew. With the need to act quickly, since during these first few hours at sea *RABASKA* was already overpowered, I moved up onto the deck to help Henk reef the sail. This was my first experience attempting to put a reef in the mainsail of *RABASKA*. Although I understood reefing procedures, this was no jiffy system and I was not pleased with how long it took and how difficult it was under the current sea conditions. I felt like an old time sailor high on the spar of a square-rigger as we tried to secure the lowered portion of the mainsail to the boom. Unfortunately, the reefing lines were all the same color but of different shapes, and getting the ends of the same line together proved to be a difficult task with the sail flapping above our heads and the wet deck pitching under our feet.

When we finally finished this task and worked our way back to the cockpit and the shelter of the dodger, it was then a simple matter to reduce the size of the jib sail as all its lines led back from the self-furling forestay.

Finally, with both sails reduced in size, the boat moved more gently, and as I relaxed from the exertion on deck, I realized the sun was beginning to set over the land. With the setting sun, the temperature also began to dip noticeably.

We had discussed the night watches and I realized it was going to take a few days to get accustomed to two hours on watch and four hours below during the night. The day watches, since we thought we would all be on deck anyway, were to be decided as required.

That first night I had been assigned a later watch, so I decided to turn in right away and get some sleep. It seemed as if I had just pulled up the sleeping bag when I was awakened by the whine of a loud engine. I knew it was not our engine, and I jumped out of my berth and rushed to the cockpit minus my tether, already breaking our steadfast rule. Suddenly our boat was encompassed in a bright light that blinded us in the dark. I thought my worst nightmare was already being realized, and some huge ship was about to cut us down. However as our eyes adjusted, the shadow of a fishing boat emerged behind the light. Henk and Peter began to shout a warning, but the boat continued to move in on us and then suddenly the search light went out and the vessel steered to starboard and circled around us. When our eyes adjusted to the darkness, we could see the huge steel beams pushed out on both sides of its stern, as it continued to drag its nets in the water. I was not sure exactly what kind of fishing trawler it was, but as my eyes adjusted to the night, I could see similar boats off in the distance. We tried calling on the radio, but we did not get a response and soon she moved off into the darkness. If the skipper was trying to scare us, he succeeded.

I thought other vessels at sea would at least acknowledge the presence of a nearby boat. This was a commercial fishing vessel and we were probably just another obstacle in his way.

The presence of these fishing trawlers brought to mind the perfect storm that swept up the Eastern Seaboard of North America in 1991. That storm was not even given a name at first for fear that it would alarm local residents. It was huge and consisted of a hurricane heading north from Bermuda, a storm heading south from Sable Island and a cold front heading east. The newspapers at the time reported waves ten storeys high and winds of 120 miles per hour or 193 kph. It finally came ashore along the Nova Scotia coast. In 2000 a movie, *The Perfect Storm* with George Clooney, depicted the tragic loss of a fishing vessel the *ANDREA GAIL* out of Gloucester, MA, a boat similar to the ones that were near us that night.

WHEN I CAME ON deck the second time that night, I noticed that it was still possible to see tiny glimmering lights along the shore of Long Island Sound. There were also a number of fishing boats visible because of their bright working lights. Those lights blocked out the boats' running lights making it difficult to see in what direction they were moving. Hence, during my two hour watch, I had to keep track of the trawlers to be sure they were staying well clear of us.

I had no sooner made myself comfortable, now snugly cocooned in my survival suit, watch cap and gloves, when we were buzzed by two jet helicopters. They also circled us, as had the fishing boat, and bathed us in bright lights as they hovered directly over us for a minute or two. I was beginning to feel as if we were some kind of phenomenon on the ocean and everyone wanted a good look at us.

On Sunday morning, our second day at sea, I watched the sun come up over the horizon and it appeared that we were in for a great day of sailing. For the most part, with Long Island off in the far, far distance, it was as if we were sailing on Lake Ontario. The movement of the boat was much like sailing at home; the color of the water, the wave patterns and wind blowing between fifteen and eighteen knots. The air however, was very cold and it was necessary to stay huddled behind the dodger where it was pleasantly warm.

When I came off watch and had a chance to get some rest I decided to take the opportunity to bake some bread and muffins using the galley stove. I had after all signed on as deck hand and cook, so it was time to get to know the galley. I had purchased an oven thermometer in a hardware store in Tarrytown. It was designed to sit on the oven grill, facing through the glass of the oven door. My recipe had called for a warm dry place to let the bread rise prior to putting it in the oven. The only place on *RABASKA* that met that criterion was the oven itself! With the heat on as low as possible, I put the pans containing the bread and muffin mix in the oven to let the dough rise. But with the motion of the boat, my precious thermometer soon disappeared somewhere in the back of the oven leaving me with no way to monitor the temperature. As I occasionally peeked into the oven, I also discovered that the side of the pan closest to the gas flame tended to burn because the boat was heeled over in that direction. The side near the oven door away from the flame did not cook nearly as well. Although the bread loaf turned out rather small, the crew appreciated both items.

We were visited by some curious sharks while we were enjoying our lunch at noon. One came up close to the boat to look us over. There would be no dangling of feet over the side that day, even if it did warm up later. At first sighting we thought the sharks might have been dolphins, but when they got close to the boat we could see their size, the gray color, the gill slits behind the head, and the erect dorsal fin that rarely protruded above the surface of the water. Perhaps they had caught a whiff of my baking and were hoping for some treats! They must have told their friends about our presence as later that same afternoon two more sharks approached us cautiously from the stern of the boat. Toward evening, and to confirm our identification of the sharks, a school of dolphins approached the boat. By comparison, we were sure that our first visitors were indeed sharks. The dolphins, on the other hand, were smaller and more friendly and playful around the boat.

The dolphin family is closely related to whales and porpoises. Like whales they breathe through a blowhole at the top of their head and as they travel, they tend to break through the surface about every two or three minutes to exhale and inhale before submerging again. They drive themselves through the water with an up/down motion of the tail and they use their flippers for stabilization. They are able to move much faster than *RABASKA,* so keeping up with our six or seven knots was not a problem for them.

Although the dolphins were not with us all the way across the ocean, for the first two weeks we were visited two or three times every day. Perhaps it was more often, but it depended on the weather conditions whether we would spot them or not. Every school or pod seemed to follow a similar pattern when around the boat. We would first identify them about a hundred yards off the starboard side. Usually there was a group of fifteen or twenty together. They would make a few runs past the boat and then congregate near the bow, where they would compete to see who could come closest without being hit by *RABASKA*! Because they have an echolocation system similar to a bat, they are able to crowd together at high speed, sometimes as much as fifteen or twenty miles per hour, and not run into each other or us. Usually when they would come around, one of us would holler, "Dolphin, Dolphin" in the hope that they would hear us. Over time, observing them was for me a peaceful and spiritual experience.

This was the first full day at sea and it became apparent that the mast was not properly jammed into its position through the coach-house roof. The wooden pegs and rubber doorstoppers we inserted back in Tarrytown soon worked themselves free. The relaxed mast was beginning to grind and creak as it moved back and forth with the motion of the boat. In the beginning, the noise did not get on our nerves. However, it did not bode well for the future.

That Sunday evening we had our first dinner at sea. The weather was still perfect, we were making good time through the water, the self-steering device was functioning well and we were free to enjoy our afternoon sail as if we were at home on Lake Ontario.

To make it a perfect day the cook prepared dinner in the late afternoon. We had fresh pork chops with apple sauce, a medley of fresh vegetables and a glass of red wine. Because of the heel of the boat, we knew it would not be possible to make use of the table in the cabin so we had planned to lap our meals in the cockpit. This meant that some balancing was required and each of us had to be especially careful where we put our glass of wine so it would not spill. The only drawback to this first dinner on-board was that as the sun went over the horizon, the temperature quickly began to drop as it did the night before. Nevertheless, it was a pleasant start and our sprits were high as we cruised into the night. In fact, Peter turned to me and said, "If this is the North Atlantic, it is not too bad at all." Then he continued, "But it ain't over till it's over and the fat lady sings." He meant no disrespect to corpulent women, but merely used that expression to suggest we suspend judgment until we landed safely in Gibraltar.

So we began our second night at sea. Both Peter and Henk complained of the cold when they came below at the end of their watch. I quickly learned the value of my survival suit, which I had donned prior to going on deck. Under the suit, I had a heavy wool sweater and a large towel wrapped around my neck to keep in the body heat. Along with the special gloves and a wool watch cap, I was comfortable, but as usual, I found my time on deck psychologically long and boring.

Below deck was a different story. Our bodies had not yet adjusted to the rhythm of the sea and the constant motion of the boat. We would roll back and forth in the berth rendering it almost impossible to get sleep. Added to this discomfort was the increasing noise the mast was making. In the still of the night, with the boat rocking rather heavily, the moans and groans of the moving mast were jarring on the nerves.

Although the land had receded at the end of the first full day at sea, I noticed during my mid watch that it was still possible to see lights in the far, far distance and off to port. I figured the lights were on the notorious Shoals of Nantucket that are known and feared by most coastal navigators. The closest light to us was probably from the 70-foot-high lighthouse situated on the Davis South Shoal. Although our course was to run along the 40th parallel of latitude, we were actually off course and on a starboard tack. I felt we were being driven in the direction of the shoals. I knew, come daylight, we would have to make an adjustment to bring us down closer to the rhumb line. However, I decided the danger was distant enough to let the other two crewmembers enjoy their sleep, if they were sleeping!

Although we were well equipped with a GPS, Peter was also keeping a daily track of our progress on a paper chart as back-up.

In the early days, on the old sailing vessels, sailing directions were oral instructions that were passed on from pilot to pilot. Eventually of course, they became written descriptions of costal navigation. From those written instructions, charts were made by the English with copious copying from the Dutch masters.

Chapter 10

Aₜₜₑᵣ A RESTLESS SLEEP I arrived on deck Monday morning to be greeted by a strong wind coming in from the southeast, which was creating a very interesting swell. I suddenly realized we were no longer sailing on Lake Ontario, even though out of habit, we continued to refer to the ocean those first few days as the lake.

The pounding of the boat into the waves made it impossible for me to attempt cooking breakfast. It was a good thing that I had baked fresh muffins on Sunday, but I managed somehow to make some fresh coffee to go with them. After a long cold night taking turns on watch, a hot coffee and muffins were an instant hit with the crew.

The southeast wind continued to blow strongly and not only drove us even further off our desired course but closer to the dangerous shoals. The lighthouses we saw during the night indicated that they were somewhere ahead of us. We tried to stay well offshore, which was no longer visible, but the wind and the waves insisted on driving us in that treacherous direction. I could see the skipper was beginning to show some concern. Finally, we decided to change direction and come off our starboard tack in order to gain more sea room. Faced with such a long journey, it was natural to feel some disappointment that we were not heading directly toward our destination. However, that is a common angst for sailors when the wind is in their face. But the disappointment was more poignant in this circumstance as it seemed we could not let go of North America to be set free in the ocean. There is no doubt that the new tack, the overcast sky and the heavy swells, dampened our spirits somewhat on this third day at sea.

I finally managed to get the stove working and prepared some hot stew for lunch. Henk had spent some time resting in the V-berth prior to lunch, even though he had decided earlier that that was not a good idea.

When he entered the main salon, he announced that he did not feel like eating. The confined space in the bow of the boat where the V-berth is located experiences the worst of the motion and he was reminded it is not a place to be for any length of time. When he appeared on deck, his face was white and sallow. It was obvious he was close to being seasick, that ancient affliction that besets those who venture to sea.

Most sailors know *mal de mer* is nothing to be ashamed of and is often a combination of food, drink, or just being in the wrong location on the boat, like the V-berth. History tells us that the great British naval hero, Lord Nelson, got sick every time he put to sea. Henk knew the importance of getting on deck and into the fresh air as soon as possible. It worked, and he was able to avoid further complications.

All three of us had experienced rough weather on Lake Ontario at one time or another. Many years ago, I was racing a small boat in an overnight long distance race. By midnight, the wind direction and the fetch had combined to create rare twenty-foot waves in the middle of the lake. However, there were no swells to complicate the condition.

Waves are a local response to the friction of the wind on the surface of the water. They often have peaks that break up periodically. But on *RABASKA,* we were discovering a new sensation. We had to deal as well with powerful swells that almost lifted the boat out of the water. You could see a bird sitting on top of the water and a huge swell would come along but the bird would remain in the same location on the surface of the water. A swell, unlike a wave, is not caused by the local conditions as we experienced on Lake Ontario, but by a storm often hundreds of miles away. The energy created moves from particle to particle, transferring its energy without affecting the surface water, as does the wind. Hence, for the first time we had both waves and swells bouncing our little boat around as we headed further out to sea.

Unlike the bird on the water that simply rode up and down on the swells, our boat was rolling from side to side and pitching bow to stern like a seesaw. When the boat was quartered by the oncoming waves, the pitch and the roll blended into a motion called yawing. I had hoped the lunch Peter and I had eaten earlier, would not decide to go for a swim in the ocean, or worse still, all over the cockpit floor.

The waves were building to ten feet and we decided to put another reef in the mainsail. When the wind was coming over the side of the boat, it was possible to make good time even without the mainsail. But when we were tacking, beating up into the wind, *RABASKA* had to have some mainsail set to give the boat drive through the water. We also decided to take off the large foresail, called a genoa or number one, and replace it with a small working jib, called the number two.

Changing a sail on the foredeck was not a simple exercise. Our genoa had to be lowered onto a pitching deck that was taking water over the pulpit. It was a large sail and gathering it together on the deck, as the wind fought desperately to blow it into the water, was a challenge. As Henk and I worked on the slippery surface, the spindrift was soaking us making it more difficult to control the situation. We had to shout to each other to be heard, and Peter, beyond reach of our voices, had to depend on our hand signals as he stood at the helm. Once we had doused the number one, we had to fold it somehow in order to get it back into the cockpit without losing it overboard.

In a similar situation on the lake, we would simply open the fore hatch and stuff the sail down into the V-berth. During my racing days, I had many very wet sails shoved into my face, as I tried to grab some sleep when off watch on a long distance race.

This maneuver was impossible on *RABASKA*. Not only would it have been very dangerous given the amount of water coming over the bow, but we had bolted the fore hatch shut to prevent waves from forcing it open and filling the boat with water.

We had to inch along the slanting deck on the low side of the pitching boat, moving our safety lines as we went, and drag that huge bundle of wet sail to the stern. We did not do a good job folding the sail, but we stuffed it in one of the back lockers anyway. Gathering our courage we then reversed the procedure, and carried the number two sail forward to the pulpit where we proceeded to pull the smaller sail out of its bag and feed it into the slot on the forestay. Sitting in the pulpit in the very bow of the boat under those conditions was like riding a wild horse backwards. As the boat plunged down the waves and over the swells, my body was lifted off the deck, became airborne for a few moments, and then I fell back into my perch against the bow rail. If it were not for the pulpit and the safety tether, I would have been swept over the bow and into the water. The rule for survival not only on deck but in the cabin as well was one hand for you and the other for the boat. Working the sail into position required me to attach the tack to the self-furling mechanism, secure the halyard to the head of the sail, and be sure the sail itself was free to be pulled up the stay. Most of these tasks had to be completed with one hand. It was not the quickest way to finish the task, but I am still here to talk about it! Meanwhile Henk tied the jib lines to the clew of the sail and led them back to the cockpit. Peter then tightened the sheets and Henk, hunkered at the foot of the mast, pulled the sail up with the halyard.

My survival suit with its safety harness gave me the confidence I needed to do this dangerous work. Under those conditions, my light weather two-piece suit would not have been able to fend off the large quantities of water searching for every possible orifice in my clothing.

PRIOR TO OUR DEPARTURE I considered what clothes to pack. My experience of traveling has not cured my penchant to take more clothes than needed. When I am not sure of the weather, I tend to pack for all seasons. I figured that since we were heading out on the North Atlantic, I would require plenty of warm clothing. Peter suggested that I should take old clothes that could be thrown away at the end of the trip. I rooted through our ragbag at home and found old T-shirts and underwear that would serve the purpose and could be discarded when they were no longer fit to wear. Although we did not change that often, we did manage to leave a few items of clothing at the bottom of the ocean.

Along with the old clothes, I realized I also wanted to purchase a good survival suit, its prime purpose being deck wear. I needed something that was not just water resistant, but water proof. I searched around the various stores in Toronto and finally found one for a price I was willing to pay. These suits are very expensive but well worth the investment. I settled on a one-piece, bright red Mustang Ocean Class suit that had built-in flotation devices and a safety harness. The shop sold it below asking price because the store owner said it was overkill for Lake Ontario and he was happy to get it off the rack. It was lined and had Velcro straps on the wrists, arms and legs, as well as pockets for a strobe light, dye marker and whistle. It came equipped with a blow-up collar to support the head in the water. The company even provided me with a stitched name tag that some friends suggested was for body identification purposes! As well as the suit, I purchased large neoprene fishing gloves equipped with Velcro that reached almost to my elbows.

To complete my attire I also included a heavy wool sweater, watch cap, a reflector hood and rubber deck boots. I was prepared for whatever Mother Nature had in store.

The rest of my wardrobe was limited to one good pair of long pants, a shirt and clean underwear for the plane ride home. These I safely stored in a plastic container in the bottom of my sea bag. Finally, in my toilet kit I included a large supply of Wet Ones Moist Wipes for body washing, and of course, lots of sunscreen for those wonderful hot days on the water that never materialized. My Mustang Survival Suit, my *house*, was the best purchase I made.

WITH THE SAILS TRIMMED and Henk and I back safely in the cockpit, we were able to come about and return to a starboard tack much closer to our course of 110°. This time we hoped it would take us well offshore and away from the fearsome shoals that had been hounding us for the past two days.

Meanwhile, the cockpit was not exactly a dry ground for Peter either. Once we had reset the sails on the foredeck, the self-steering Monitor had to be readjusted to the new conditions. To make those changes, Peter had to leave the safety of the cockpit and step out on the stern of the boat for his own baptism in salt water. It was not as dangerous as working on the bow perhaps, but it was still not a nice place to be. Finally, as we hunkered down again under the dodger to take a rest, all three of us looked as if we had been swimming in our wet gear.

Even though the sun was peeking through the clouds, a low clinging fog started to roll in over the water. These were the conditions I disliked, and to make matters worse our new tack put us once again in the middle of the shipping lanes out of New York. To compound the situation our current location and personal discomfort were already having a negative effect on our morale. We felt that the adverse conditions were holding us back from where we wanted to go. If a situation like that persisted on Lake Ontario, we probably would have lowered the sails, turned on the motor, and headed home, or at least to the nearest port, a good stiff drink, a hot meal and a dry berth.

When Peter told some of his friends that he was planning to cross the ocean, someone asked him where he would be staying at night! Unfortunately, you quickly learn there are no marinas or safe harbors to drop into at dusk. We had to carry on under the current conditions.

Suddenly we found ourselves in a cluster of red floating net markers. The Monitor was steering the boat and before we could adjust the direction, we ran over one of them. I was afraid we would end up with the fishing net attached to the keel, or even worse wrapped around our rudder or propeller. Luckily, neither of these things happened, but Henk was prepared and jumped on deck, knife in hand, ready to cut us loose.

By 1700, we were still on the same tack and under reduced sail but the waves had built to a height of twelve feet. I wanted to get a picture of the waves to take back home at the end of the trip, but it was impossible to capture their awesome beauty. Just when the wave looked enormous and ready to encompass us, the boat would suddenly rise to meet the challenge, and the camera captured what looked like a five-foot wave. I figured the only way to get a telling picture of the wave would be from a distance. I was not in the mood to go swimming simply to prove to a friend that I was telling the truth.

DURING THE DAY, I had the opportunity to watch the birds that were flying near the boat. It is a wonderful sight to see them in flight, to rise up over the crest of a wave, only to glide down the other side into the trough. These acrobatic birds were able to feed on small fish, plankton and minerals that were close to the surface. Like true sailors, the ocean was their home and they only returned to land to breed on some inaccessible island. I envied their freedom and their ability to fly and glide with such little effort. But I also found them a comfort and associated them with the land, the land that was now two hundred miles behind us.

The wind and the waves continued to beat against us and our progress through the water was sluggish. Henk decided it would be a good idea to shake out one of the reefs in the mainsail to get more drive in the water. We were still flying the number two and the main was now double reefed. I did not agree with this assessment, but I stuck to my resolve not to interfere with the skipper's decisions, unless I felt my own life was in danger. This was my contribution to on-board harmony. However, Henk and Peter discussed the idea and it was decided to take the main down altogether for the night. I liked that decision. It was in my opinion the safer choice and it meant less hassle if the night watch had to wake up crew to shorten sail.

However, we were concerned with the deteriorating condition of the mast. The shrill creaks coming from that direction became more and more piercing. It was swaying back and forth in its perch. The squeals and groans were loud enough to be heard on deck in spite of the raging wind and rolling waves. It meant the load on the mast was shifting and putting undue stress on the shrouds and stays. The pegs that we had driven into place to steady the mast kept popping out as the mast worked them loose. The skipper would go below, gather the supports off the cabin floor and drive them back up into the space between the mast and the coach-house roof. But no matter how often he drove them into position, it was only a matter of time before they popped out again, and the squeals re-commenced their nerve-shattering ruckus.

Since I was not on watch, I decided it was time to go to the galley and get dinner. In spite of the motion below, I did manage to cook balsamic chicken for the crew. I realized as I worked in the galley that I had a lot to learn about getting meals on a small boat in motion. There had to be a way of bracing myself so that I would have two hands free to work the tiny old army can opener Henk had found somewhere, without releasing my hold on the boat! It was dangerous even to let go for a moment, as a sudden shift in the boat's movement could throw me across to the other side of the cabin.

Even if I did manage to successfully open a can by sitting on the floor and using both hands as I slid around, where would I put it so that it would not disappear or spill all over? If I put it on the counter top, it would have been on the floor in seconds. In those conditions, fiddles around the edge of the table, meant to hold things in place when the boat is heeling over, might have been helpful. I seemed to spend more time mopping up spills and chasing dishes and pots around the galley, than I did actually getting dinner ready. I had to figure out how to survive in the galley, or I would have to abandon my beautiful fourteen-day menu and start serving food directly out of the cans.

Chapter 11

I TURNED IN RIGHT AFTER dinner and returned to the deck again for my 0200 watch. The waves were running at close to twenty feet but the steering Monitor was doing a splendid job of keeping the boat on course. In the dark, you could hear the water rushing along the side of the boat and it gave me the feeling that we were now finally making good progress in the right direction.

The deck noises at night were like those made by a very steep rocky mountain river in the forest. The water was constantly breaking over the bow and then cascading along both sides of the boat, to be sucked into the scupper holes. This caused a loud noise like someone trying to get the last of their drink through a huge straw. But as the boat rode up the next wave, the escaping water was blocked by the surface water being forced up from the bottom. This process caused a large geyser on each side of the boat that sounded like blowing and sucking in alternating rhythm. If nothing else, it helped to keep the crew awake during their watch. As the boat rode up one side of the wave it then sped down the other side at remarkable speeds, with twelve knots often showing on the knot meter (not the GPS average speed over the ground!). In this totally black environment, it was better than any midway ride I have ever experienced.

As I sat alone in the middle of the night, the impression I had in the pitch-dark cockpit differed from what I knew was really happening. It felt as if the boat was climbing up one side of the wave, leveling off for a moment, and then starting up the next wave. We seemed to be climbing higher and higher, as if we were moving constantly uphill. Although I knew the boat was speeding down the other side of the wave, that strange motion for some reason was not that obvious to me. It was the first time I ever climbed a pair of stairs while sitting in a thirty-seven-foot boat. Cripes, I thought I was losing it already!

As I sat in the cockpit, feet braced against the hull and my back pushed hard against the bulkhead, I noticed that the clouds had parted for a moment and the moon appeared through the mist for the first time. I looked up at that beautiful natural satellite and said, "I love you" to Maureen who was probably sound asleep at home.

We live on the twentieth floor on the west side of a condominium and it is possible, while lying in bed at night, to see the moon through the huge window at the foot of the bed. I knew that moon was visible to her and hoped that she was awake and thinking of me as it shined through her window and cast its light across our bed.

Moments later the moon and the few stars that were visible disappeared. The magic moment was gone. I knew then that if the same weather conditions persisted, not only would I lose contact with Maureen, but also we would never be able to enjoy the stars and learn more about celestial navigation. I was hoping to learn that art on the trip and we had brought along the sextant and the reference charts. But it would have been impossible even if the stars were visible, to sight them when all our energy was required to hold on and keep the boat moving toward our destination.

When Peter arrived on deck at 0400 to take over the watch, I decided to make some hot coffee. He looked as if he needed something to help him through the watch. Below deck resembled the inside of a washing machine. It seemed as if the boat itself did not want us in the cabin. It was next to impossible to keep your feet on the damp, slippery floor. If there was some constant pattern to the motion then it would have been a little easier to move about. But just when you thought you had figured out the boat's next move, it changed, and you found you had to hold on with an even tighter grip.

Needless to say, it was difficult and dangerous to boil water under those conditions. A good scalding was a real possibility. If I had lost my balance, I could have splashed the scalding water not only on my hands, but possibly over Henk who was trying to sleep in the nearby quarter berth.

I finally managed to put two cups of coffee together and before handing up a steaming cup to Peter on deck, I thought we could both use a little schnapps to go with it. I added a dollop of rum to each mug.

I then joined Peter in the cockpit and realized that somehow or other, we were beginning to adjust to the harsh conditions. But at the same time, they were taking their toll on our bodies. Our major activity when not on watch was to try sleep in the nearest berth.

EVEN AS WE SLEPT our bodies were not getting a proper rest. The constant shifting of the boat kept the semiconscious body in motion, and the huge waves noisily crashing on the deck coupled with the squawking mast, intruded into our subconscious. I noticed how none of us needed to be called to sit our watch, and how the slightest change in the elements would interrupt the hibernating crewmembers in their sleeping bags. This may explain why we were always tired and dropped into an empty berth as soon as we went below.

One of the truths I learned quickly was that the simplest things we do on shore, such as shaving, become major tasks on a small boat in a rough sea. I always thought when I saw recreational sailors returning from their conquest that the beard was meant to reinforce the tough male image. It carried the visible message, "I went to sea and survived." However, I soon learned to put that preconceived notion behind me. I suppose it was possible even if extremely difficult, to shave in our current situation. But in my opinion to attempt to shave, even with a safety razor, would be akin to inviting suicide. Besides, what would be the point of shaving? Who cares what you look like—certainly the other members of the crew don't care! But I must admit I did notice that Peter and Henk were already beginning to look rather seedy!

The daily bathroom ablutions and other duties performed in that sacred place, which are routinely and easily completed on land, take on a new challenge in a bouncing boat.

I should point out that it would have been a mistake to spend too much time in the head at any rate, since it was near the bow of the boat and any prolonged confinement to that area was likely to bring on a sudden bout of seasickness. I saw a few gray faces suddenly appear on deck after a visit to the head that first week. The simple task of brushing my teeth took twenty to thirty minutes in the confines of that cramped quarters. Keeping myself properly braced and at the same time, executing a particular duty was an open invitation to a nasty accident. Indeed that is what I experienced just after breakfast one day.

Before leaving New York we switched the head from a holding tank to pumping the contents through a macerator and overboard. Since boat toilets are all unique it takes some time learning the foibles of different systems. Water and waste sloshing around under your bare ass increases the area to be wiped and dried, thus requiring extra tissue. Two valves had to be opened to use the head properly. One valve allowed salt water in, if the boat was not heeling over too far, and the other valve emptied the contents of the macerator out through the hull of the boat and into the ocean. It was necessary to open these valves hidden in an awkward position under the sink and to close them when the operation was complete. Toilet paper can be both a blessing and a curse in a boat's head. Normally the bowl rule is nothing goes into it that has not first passed through the body. But on *RABASKA,* paper was permitted while at sea. However, the overuse of paper can clog the small pipes making it difficult to flush the contents overboard. I found this out the hard way. Having completed my task one day and managing to get my pants up around my waist without falling over, I began to pump the bowl dry. I had used too much paper in the drying process and the paper blocked the valve after one short pump. When I drew the handle back for a second try the boat flew over a wave and came down hard on the water forcing the contents of the bowl upwards. I cannot repeat my language here but the crew in the cockpit got an earful. Not only was I wearing the mess on my face, but it spattered on the walls and floor of the head as well. With no fresh water immediately available, it was a major task to pump clear the toilet, get myself cleaned up, and attempt to wash down the surrounding walls. All this had to be done while the boat continued to pitch and toss. As a result of this experience, I learned to pump lots of seawater into the bowl, even if it did splash around under me, so that the contents would move through the system without an argument. The fact my bottom got wet in the process did not make a big difference as it was damp most of the time anyway. I think I learned enough those first few days to qualify for a spot in *Cirque du Soleil.*

Similar gymnastics were also required when making a change of clothing, donning sea boots and especially attempting to get damp feet into a pair of dry socks, if any could be found.

LATE IN THE AFTERNOON of day four the storm finally abated but the swells did not relax. In fact the wind got so quiet we decided to roll in the jib and in its place to fly a very light and colorful sail called a DRS. This sail can only be used in light wind and a relatively flat sea. It clipped onto the bow with an adjustable pulley and then the sail was hoisted on a spare halyard. One sheet is all that is necessary to hold the sail in place.

Even though the wind had diminished significantly, I felt the motion of the boat over the large swells would make it difficult to control. The boom swung back and forth and the sails made a thunderous salvo. Because there was not enough wind to hold them in place they flopped from side to side, and the noise became agonizing. It was also a concern that the motion would break down the fiber in the sail.

We were now in a similar situation although it was a pleasant change from what we had been experiencing. The severe rocking motion was aggravating the stability of the mast even more, and we eventually had to lower the mainsail and secure the boom. In spite of my initial misgiving, the DRS began to take hold and the Monitor did a great job as we slowly moved forward.

Just before nightfall, we lowered the DRS and ran the motor for forty-five minutes to recharge our batteries. It was a harsh sound. We had become accustomed to the rhythm and noises of sailing. We all gave a sigh of relief when the engine was finally shut off and the small jib was reset for the night.

Chapter 12

It was my turn for what would normally be called the middle watch, from 0000 to 0400. Because there were only three of us, we did not use the traditional watch assignments. Since we knew we would be up and about during the daylight hours, no specific watch times were set. As well, we varied the night watches so that no one would be stuck with the same assignment for the whole trip. We were, as mentioned, on deck for two hours and off four hours repeatedly throughout the night. Hence, the daytime was often the best opportunity to catch up on sleep. So rather than four hours for the middle watch, I was only responsible for the first two hours of that watch. On a vessel that is fully crewed the first and last dog watches are often split into two hours each so that the same sailors are not always on duty at the same time.

I found it difficult to struggle into my suit and to find things in the dark without disturbing Peter who, judging by the sound of his snoring, was finally enjoying a good sleep. The wind had abated somewhat again, but there were no stars. I figured we would have rain before daybreak. Henk was happy to leave the watch and head for his bunk.

Our bearing was 120° but we had fallen 85 nautical miles off course. We had to hold the boat close to the wind, and this continued to make the situation in the cabin even more uncomfortable. I was happy to see Peter poke his head up through the hatch two hours later. Because of the high sea, we had been keeping the hatch cover closed to prevent water getting below. Neither Peter nor Henk had a problem opening the hatch from below, but I found it rather difficult. If I gave it a good bang with the heel of my hand, it would slide back. However, I was reluctant to do that for fear of awakening whoever was sleeping at the time. It was also difficult to get the heavy hatch boards back into place when the boat was in constant motion. I understood the need to keep the boat closed up, but I was concerned about getting out in a hurry if that was necessary. Closing up the boat this way also made the night watches even more isolated, and it was a happy sound when I heard the hatch sliding back and another face appearing to take over the watch. As I said before, I dislike night watches.

I went off watch at 0200 only to be awakened again at 0600 for my half of the morning watch. This was the beginning of our fifth day at sea and the boat was moving through a series of rainsqualls. Peter remained on deck and we could look around and see about a dozen storm squalls out on the bulging ocean. They were shaped like giant mushrooms and we observed them moving across the surface of the water. The conversation tended to dwell on the squalls and we discussed which ones we could avoid and which ones we would have to sail through. It was like playing tag with the weather. That morning we sailed through five major squalls and finally when Henk came on deck, we decided it was necessary to reduce sail even further to prevent damage to the boat's equipment.

I rather enjoyed the squalls as each one gave us fair warning and it was fun guessing which ones would jump on us and which would quickly pass us by. They broke the monotony of sailing where there was such a lack of visual variety. I have read many times the term *the lonely sea* and now I came to know the full meaning of that expression. To experience the vastness of the water day after day, when our position in the waterscape seemed to remain fixed, made us believe that we were making no progress at all. Every day the vista was a repeat of the day before. There was nothing new or nothing different visually. I felt like a Lilliputian sitting in the middle of a long-playing record. The only thing I could see was the horizon, or the edge of the record, in every direction. There was nothing to break the monotony. I could stand up and look over the dodger, slowly turning my body 360°, and what I saw was the same unbroken line where the sky and water meet. A day with many squalls, even if the wind shifts were dramatic, was a day very different from all others—a day to enjoy.

During that day along with the line squalls, we were again visited by some sharks, dolphins and those magnificent flying machines, the birds that live over the water.

The storms continued all day. In the afternoon, I sat on the berth on the port side and spoke quietly into a tape recorder. Henk was trying to get some sleep in the quarter berth. It had been, in simple words, another wild day. The sea was angry and the weather was angrier still. We had the boat under control and the sails properly trimmed for the conditions. With a reef in the main and the working jib rolled down to half its normal size, we were trucking along at seven knots. Peter, I discovered, has a knack for trimming the sails and balancing the boat. We covered thirty-five miles in five hours, which means we were making excellent progress. The boat was driving forward and we could hear every timber straining as we surged through the sea.

Off and on all day in spite of the weather, we had schools of dolphins running along beside us. I tried calling them. I don't know if they paid any attention to me, but again I cried, "Dolphin, Dolphin" as they came close to the boat before they ended up under the surge of the bow. Once they were there the sailing conditions made it too dangerous to go forward, as I did on the first day we encountered them.

The weather remained extremely uncomfortable. On top of the high wind, rainsquall after rainsquall came down on us constantly challenging our sailing skills. In the early part of the day, they were definitely exciting to watch, but as the day moved forward, they became a nuisance. Fortunately for us, Peter preferred to be on deck in those conditions. During the day, he often remained there for hours, giving Henk and me a break below. The self-steering Monitor worked very well. It was like having a fourth crewmember who needed neither food nor rest, and who could stand watch for days on end. But the Monitor was only a splendid coxswain as long as it was supported by the eyes of a mariner on deck.

The waves continued to sweep over the boat, and one of them almost washed the dodger off the coach-house roof. Without the dodger, life on deck would have become acutely uncomfortable. When Henk had a new dodger made for the trip, the manufacturer failed to cut the lower edge properly. There was a two-inch space at one point where it fitted along the edge of the deck. Sitting too close to that spot guaranteed a wet back in no time. To have the whole dodger removed by a wave would have been the elimination of what little comfort there was on deck. The cockpit would have become a constant well full of water.

LATER THAT SAME DAY we had to reduce the working jib even further, but the boat continued to drive forward. In spite of the uncomfortable conditions, we took solace in the fact that we were moving with determination toward our destination.

As the wind shifted, we began to experience a problem with the self-steering Monitor. Part of the Monitor was an arm that extended out about one foot over the stern. On the end of this arm there was a lead counterbalance. When we sailed too close to the wind the counter weight hit against the stern pulpit. With the severe motion of the boat, it was not a gentle blow, and we were afraid the vane would be damaged. This condition also forced the boat off course because the vane could not operate freely. Like the loss of the dodger, the absence of the Monitor would also impose great hardship on the crew. A number of solutions were discussed. One of them was to take a hacksaw and cut a piece out of the stern pulpit. This would have created a major problem in turn, for it would weaken the whole system of lifelines that depended on the bow pulpit and stern pulpit for stability. We finally decided to wait till we reached the Azores before any major repairs were attempted.

In spite of the line squalls that day, the howling wind, the flying rain in our faces and the water coming over the boat, the barometer remained steady. This was a clear indication that the situation was not going to get worse. It was also evident that it would not be a dry or pleasant night on watch.

After lunch, I tried to do some reading for the first time. I was now getting enough rest so that I could spend some of my off-watch doing something other than cooking and sleeping. I found I could read and the motion did not cause the beginning of *mal de mer*. When I looked up from my book, Peter was peering down at me through the open part of the hatch. He was wrapped in his oilskins, water dripping down his five-day beard, and he said, "Well, would you look at Mr. Grannan? He thinks he's on vacation. He's sitting there reading a book while the rest of us are hanging on by the skin of our teeth." I did not think the word vacation was the appropriate one, but I was happy that I was now able to read some of the novels I had brought along for the cruise. Actually, I only read for a short time, as I wanted to build up my tolerance and to adjust my eyes gradually to the motion. I was pleased that I now had another option when off duty.

BEFORE LEAVING ON THIS trip, an experienced ocean sailor told me that the most exciting moment each day was the dinner in the evening. This was not to be. I had hoped the crew would gather at dinner time in the salon to eat and not just to take turns drinking the water off a newly opened can of vegetables! On the other hand, it must have been entertaining to watch me chase the food and dishes around the galley.

For dinner that evening, I decided to use up the last of our fresh meat. Without refrigeration or ice, the little bit of fresh meat that was left would soon have to go overboard, if not cooked. So I cooked up the meat and served it along with the remaining fresh vegetables. We had two apples, lots of onions, a few potatoes and two carrots left. We were getting near the end of our fresh supplies. The eggs were surviving the ride quite well. From then on, we had to depend on canned goods, rice or pasta. The hot stew that night, in spite of the age of the meat, was excellent, if I say so myself. There was enough left over for lunch the following day.

I still had a great deal of difficulty in the galley. There, as in the head, simple operations continued to become major challenges. I was constantly attempting to balance pots on the stove or on the counter top. I thought again about some fiddles on the counter to keep things in place. I even tried to make something with pieces of wood and clamps, but there was no way even that would keep the food items in place. Each food item then, had to be cooked separately and then stored in some safe location where it would remain relatively hot until I got the next item opened and cooked. I finally had to give up the stove and attempted to do all the cooking and boiling in the propane pressure cooker. This Sea Cook was specifically designed for the conditions we were experiencing. It was mounted on the bulkhead near the companionway and was gimballed to assure ease of swing. Unfortunately, the cookbook for the pressure cooker had been lost. In the beginning, I had to experiment with the timing for each food item. Peter did not like me using the pressure cooker at first because he had heard about the possibility of unwarranted explosions. Henk assured both of us that his cooker had a number of safety valves. Nevertheless, in our rough conditions I had to brace myself carefully and hold on to the cooker with oven mitts until the cooking was complete. If I let the steam off in the galley, the inside of the boat became unbearable with the added moisture. To avoid this problem I would hand the cooker up to Henk on deck. He would then steady the pot on the bench as I reached up to trip the release valve.

I found the sink was the best place to set down any cooked items. The sides of the sink kept things relatively steady and if there was any spillage, it would go out through the drain in the bottom. If it was not too rough and we were on a port tack, I could prop things on the low side of the counter top and have some confidence they would not end up on the deck. But even there they did tend to spill when we went over the bumps in the road.

In spite of the difficulties in the galley, I stuck to my resolve to continue to produce the meals that I had planned and to provide the crew with more than a cold can of pork sausages. Of course, I was not able to duplicate the custom of the 19th century Royal Navy. In those days, dinner was served in the Great Cabin with the Captain, who would often invite his officers and the occasional midshipman, to dine with him. Our captain had to lap his food in the cockpit in all kinds of weather with the rest of the crew. And there was no decanter of red wine to slide along the table for refills at the end of the meal.

WE GRADUALLY FELL INTO a daily routine. First and foremost was the navigation and boat handling. That early in the trip the navigation does not have to be precise. We only needed to head in the general direction. Once we got within one or two hundred miles of the Azores, we had to be accurate with our calculations. Peter's daily plotting on the chart produced a visual course that helped to contribute to the feeling that we were making some progress across the ocean.

We realized that once we got closer to land we would do the plotting on a smaller and more detailed chart. Until then the bigger chart was adequate, and it was important, especially during the night watches, to keep the boat on the compass course. It is surprising how far off course you can get in only a few short hours. With the self-steering Monitor, the boat stayed on course provided there was not a significant change in the wind direction. For this reason, it was necessary to glance at the compass often and to make appropriate adjustments to the Monitor.

My time on each watch was taken up with observing the compass, adjusting the steering-vane if necessary, making course corrections and keeping a close watch for freighters. After a while, I developed a routine that included moving from one side of the boat to the other every fifteen minutes. This way I could divide the watch into segments to break the monotony and to keep me awake.

On many occasions, some major sail trimming was necessary in order to maintain a balanced boat. I did not like making these adjustments alone at night, no matter how necessary, because they usually required some deck work as well. But when the wind perked up, major sail adjustments had to be made or *RABASKA* would become overpowered and move off the selected course. Using too much sail drove the boat further up into the wind. Even below deck when the boat was driving, I could feel it torque and twist as it fought both wind and waves. When this began to happen, the stress on the hull was tremendous and it was necessary, night or day, to reduce sail to limit the amount of hull flexing. The safest time to do that work was when the next watch came on deck.

When Peter did the daily distance calculation on the paper chart, it became apparent that if something happened during the night to slow down the boat, we did not cover our average number of nautical miles in a twenty-four-hour period.

Below deck gradually became very damp and uncomfortable. The concept of having a cozy cabin to escape to after a long watch on deck no longer existed. Going below each time with our clothing wet from topside transported the dampness right onto our berths. However, we also discovered that the sea was finding its way into the cabin as well. It first appeared that the port side of the boat, which was the highest side out of the water most of the time, was the culprit. But the starboard side with the deck rail a few inches above the water surface was also a problem. Water was beginning to appear in the quarter berth, and it was gathering along the floorboards on the low side. When we came below and slipped out of our boots and wet clothing, our stocking feet encountered cold puddles of salty seawater. Not a comfortable feeling or a good beginning to much needed rest. We did not see the situation as serious and considered it just another inconvenience at the time.

To COMBAT THE DAMPNESS Henk turned on the Force 10 cabin heater and it appeared to dry everything below, finally making the cabin cozy and warm. We were all looking for a spot on the cabin handrails to hang a few pairs of socks and soggy T-shirts. Even though the boat was still bouncing and pitching, for some reason or other a dry cabin made it a little easier to relax and rest. I also used the opportunity of a warm cabin to change out of my dirty damp clothes for the first time. It was warm enough to take a Scotch bath using my body wipes, before putting on some dry clothes. It felt wonderful.

About midday, we sighted another sail. We were not the only ones bobbing around on this vast ocean! It looked terribly small on the horizon, so I went below to get the glasses. It soon became clear that our courses would eventually converge. I thought how ironic it would be if we were to run into each other.

As we got close, it became apparent that the other sailboat was a catamaran, a two-hulled vessel. She had very little sail flying, just a small portion of its two jibs. At first, we thought the skipper was trying to make his way over to us. He did not answer a radio call. Was his radio not working? Did he need some assistance? Given the size of the waves, I doubt there was any way we could come alongside to render aid.

As we sailed closer to each other, we realized he was hove-to, one way of slowing the boat down so it does not have to be actively steered. Had the crew been swept overboard?

When we were close enough to make out the details of the hull, Henk called again on the radio. After a long pause, we received a reply in English. It appeared that the skipper was in no danger and was probably asleep when we first called him. He informed us that the sea was too rough, as his small catamaran could not sail through the waves. He was waiting for a better day and a calmer sea. This made sense to us as heaving-to is an important maneuver for a solo sailor. To avoid exhaustion it is better to stop fighting the elements and to wait out the storm. And that was exactly what he was doing. Although he told us he had been at sea for thirty-five days, he did not require any assistance. However, I had some doubts as he then went on in a strange voice to warn us not to get too far north, or we would run into icebergs! The rambling tone of his comments and the fact he never appeared on deck, led me to believe he might have been suffering from fatigue and was somewhat confused. We decided to carry on and leave him behind on the empty sea. It was not long before his little vessel disappeared over the horizon. I did not envy him but I admired his patience. Because of his British accent, we started referring to him as British Bob.

After our encounter with British Bob, we discussed doing something about the incessant screeching of the mast. Henk continued to pound the wooden pegs up from the bottom, but one good wave would force them out soon after. We did not dare consider removing the mast collar to drive the pegs down from the top. This would have exposed the boat to the wash constantly swirling around the base of the mast. The cabin would take in too much water before we could get the job completed. So the mast continued its moaning both night and day.

Even though I had the opportunity that day to take a bath and change my clothes, I was soon reduced to my previous state. I concluded that attending to personal hygiene was waste of time. I had lost my motivation to endure the gymnastics required to achieve it for such a short time. Cleanliness was no longer a satisfying reward! Being on-board *RABASKA* had become, in a few days, an experience of living at a very basic level where personal cleanliness and intellectual stimulation were practically nonexistent, and survival had become my paramount consideration.

ON THE MORNING OF the sixth day, we were still making good time but the hostile conditions had not changed. Indeed, the previous night was one of our worst. The wind was gusting much more than forty knots and we estimated the waves to be cresting at twenty-three feet. Of course, we realized there are really no rules about waves as there are so many factors to take into consideration, for example; the wind speed, how long it has been blowing, the length of the fetch, the distance between crests and so forth. I also realize that measuring the size of a wave from a small boat is rather difficult. When I looked over the stern of the boat in the beginning of our voyage, it appeared as if the approaching wave was going to break over the stern, but it hardly ever did. It seemed to flatten out at the last minute. We did know the wind speed and were able to estimate the height of the wave using what is known as the Beaufort Scale. This system was developed in 1850 by Admiral Sir Francis Beaufort of the British Navy. He developed some guidelines that we used for our calculation. We knew we had almost unlimited fetch, the wind had been blowing for days, and according to the guidelines, we were on the edge of a strong gale. Sir Francis told us that in our current circumstance we could expect wave heights from eighteen to twenty-three feet. We also knew from experience that if you are standing in the cockpit and your eyes are about ten feet above the surface of the water, then the waves at the horizon would be approximately ten feet high. So adding our own observations, no matter how unreliable, we estimated twenty-three-foot waves. But it was hard to believe there even was an average, as some appeared much larger than that.

During the early evening, the temperature had begun to rise. Henk believed we must have crossed into the Gulf Stream. The Gulf Stream is a warm current that flows in a generally northerly direction from the Straits of Florida to the Grand Banks. Its location can vary depending on the season, but it seems to pick up off Cape Hatteras and when it reaches approximately 30°W 40°N it flows toward Europe where it is called the North Atlantic Drift. The water between the coast of the United States and the Stream, the water we had been sailing through for the past five days, is often referred to as the Cold Wall, because it is much colder than the water in the Gulf Stream. We figured we were now getting into the Stream, which is about 200 km wide. Finally, some decent weather was in store for us. It was not only warmer, but the humidity below decks had suddenly become quite noticeable. The temperature of the Stream was 25° Celsius or 77° Fahrenheit. The average current in the stream is three miles per hour so it also helped pull us back on our course. What was fascinating about the water was the sudden change in color. It was much saltier and a bright blue.

During my early night watch, which I now called black watches because the nights were so dark, I saw for the first time the phosphorescence in the water. Although the night was still pitch black, the very darkness enhanced the phosphorescence. The ocean looked like a black carpet and as the bow of the boat surged through the water, it peeled away the surface layer and threw beautiful emeralds out on each side of the boat. These stunning emeralds and pearls streamed along the gunwales, sparkling and dancing, until they disappeared in our wake.

What made this natural beauty even more intoxicating was a surprise early-evening visit by my friends the dolphins. No doubt they had visited many previous nights, but it was not possible to see them. Now as they went through their usual pattern of behavior, they created their own magnificent phosphorescent wake. The boat was surrounded by snake-like streaks of exploding pearls that created the most beautiful light show I have ever seen. It was even more wonderful when they gathered at the bow of the boat, toward the end of their cavorting, to add their luminescence to that created by the bow of *RABASKA*. No one could choreograph that performance as well as those dolphins did that night. I felt privileged that they would put on that magnificent performance just for me, alone in the cockpit, far out on the sea. It remains one of the most memorable moments in the whole voyage.

Overall, it had not been a bad day and the boat was moving at nine knots through the water most of the time. I don't think the boat could go any faster. It was surging as if impatient to get to our destination, and it gave me the impression that we were going to make this voyage in record time. But when Peter came on deck he had to remind me that, "It ain't over till it's over and the fat lady sings."

When I went below to get some sleep, I discovered why Peter reminded me of those words. I found the conditions below were continuing to deteriorate. The torque action of the hull was more obvious below than it was from the deck. In the open air, the crew's attention was riveted on keeping the sails trimmed and making sure the boat remained on course. When all three of us were on deck, we enjoyed the thrill of surging through the water and dashing toward our destination. But as soon as I went below, I realized we were pushing the boat too hard. Peter and Henk were on deck and I sat on the companionway steps, the hatch closed behind me, thinking that the boat was overpowered. I had never heard the hull complain as it seemed to be doing as I sat there. There were new creaks, groans and noises added to the ones to which we had become accustomed. The cacophony of noises made it impossible for me to lie on a bunk and catch some sleep. I had the feeling the boat was simply going to pull itself apart if we continued to drive it that hard. It was like trying to sleep in a jeep that was driving quickly over a corduroy road, every minute flying over a gully and landing heavily on the other side.

I tried to lie back and concentrate on sleeping. I was unable to relax. Soon I found myself sitting on the side of the bunk wondering what was going to happen next. I had kept my resolve not to interfere with the sailing decisions of the skipper up to this point in our journey. Peter and Henk, because they were on deck, had no idea of the punishment the boat was undergoing below deck. If one of them had come below, they would have also been alarmed. I could actually see the torque action as it moved from the bow to the stern. It was as if some giant had one hand around the bow, and another around the stern, and was twisting the whole boat back and forth trying to separate the deck from the hull and break the boat open.

After much agonizing, I finally got up off the bunk, clawed my way to the companionway, and sliding back the hatch stuck my head up into the cockpit. I simply suggested they reduce sail and explained to them that in my opinion, we were driving the boat too hard. Fortunately, they quickly agreed and to allay my concerns, shortened the jib sail. When I returned below the motion was far less stressful, both for the boat and for me, and I soon fell into a deep sleep.

Chapter 13

For safety purposes we had an inflatable rubber boat that we secured on the top deck, just behind the mast. This raft came packed in a fiberglass container, three feet by two feet, and was strapped to a holder that in turn was bolted to the deck. When inflated, it would hold four people. It was also equipped with a canopy to protect the crew from the bad weather or intense sun. If we had to abandon *RABASKA* in the ocean, the idea was to release the life raft and climb aboard. If there was no time to release it, then when the boat sank to a certain depth, the life raft would release itself and automatically inflate. This all sounds quite logical and possible. Perhaps it could work that way, but in my opinion, Lady Luck would have to play a very important role as well.

We also had a ten-foot dinghy that was deflated and stored in the rear locker along with a ten-horsepower outboard motor minus gas. Its main purpose was to be used as a tender when we reached the cruising grounds of the Mediterranean Sea.

We had an emergency pack in the port locker near the cockpit. While there were flares packed into the life raft, there was no water or food. So we had a grab bag containing a small desalinator, canned food, chocolate, an emergency first aid kit and fishing gear.

Located below deck and fastened to the base of the mast, there was a large electronic device called an EPIRB (Emergency Position Indicating Radio Beacon). This tool emits radio beacons identifying our vessel and giving our position on the sea. It was to be used only in emergencies. The instrument was registered worldwide and if it were triggered it would immediately emit a signal that could then be picked up by satellite and relayed to the nearest rescue station. We discovered there are not too many such rescue stations in the middle of the North Atlantic Ocean!

We also had a hand-held smaller model and its signal could be picked up by a passing plane or ship and then relayed to the nearest center.

I was aware that these fine electronic instruments would be of no value in an emergency unless there was a ship or another boat in the vicinity. A international law specifies that if a vessel is in trouble, a nearby boat will go to its aid. But what if there were no other vessels in the vicinity? Then the old question raises its head. If sailors wish to sail far from land and end up in trouble, should taxpayers foot the bill for a difficult and costly rescue? Often not even such a public rescue may be possible. But at the same time, if men and women had not dared to do dangerous things, would not society have lost something of great importance?

So each of us was assigned a task. In an emergency Henk was to see that the life raft was properly launched; Peter was to collect the two electronic EPIRBs and I was to grab the man-overboard emergency kit from the stern locker. Well, that was the theoretical plan on paper anyway!

Our seventh day at sea was also our first day of any physical relief. We were now definitely convinced that we were not sailing on Lake Ontario. Indeed the word lake had been completely removed from our vocabulary.

By early morning, the wind and the waves had abated, and because we had entered the Gulf Stream, the weather was a welcome change. The sun, which had been playing hide-and-seek up until now, had finally revealed itself. It was our first chance to relax and enjoy calmer seas, lighter winds and an elevated mood. We shook out both reefs in the main, and for the first time in a few days, we were sailing peacefully under full sail. On the other hand, the high winds during the past twenty-four hours had pushed us a remarkable one hundred and ninety-one miles. A record day of sailing to be sure!

The first thing we did when the sun warmed us up was to strip off our grubby clothes and treat ourselves to a saltwater shower. The warm Gulf water felt wonderful, as bucket after bucketful, sloshed over our bodies. It has been known for centuries, from the time of Hippocrates about 400 BCE in fact, that a salt bath helps relieves pain, heals cuts and produces greater mobility and relaxation. We felt wonderful as we dipped buckets over the side and dumped the warm salty water over our heads letting it run down our naked bodies. In fact, it felt so good we decided to wash our dirty laundry in the buckets as well! There was a happy mood on deck as we hung our freshly washed clothes along the lifelines on both sides of the boat. Unfortunately, as the sun dried our bodies, the refreshing water left a layer of salt residue. With no fresh water available for a rinse, an irritating discomfort remained. Rinsing with fresh water was out of the question, as our limited supply was needed for drinking and cooking. There was no warm rain shower anywhere on the horizon that would wash the white powdery film off our bodies. The wonderful benefits we felt while we frolicked under the buckets of warm salt water were somewhat diminished as our blanched skin began to dry. The cleaned clothes were impossible to wear as the dry salt, especially in our skivvies, chafed and scratched so bad it was impossible to sit down.

Because of the remarkable weather, all of the crew was on deck most of the day, enjoying the warm sun and a pleasant sail. At high noon, six dolphins joined us. I went up to the bow, something I could not normally do, and leaned over the side of the boat. I called them as I gently tapped the side of the hull. They remained much longer than usual, and I did have the feeling they were paying some attention to what I was doing. This went on for a remarkable fifteen minutes. I decided to get my camera for a picture. When I returned to the bow, camera in hand, they were still there. But as soon as I got the camera out of its case and focused, they disappeared. Dolphins must be camera shy!

Later hundreds of flying fish came out of the water about fifty yards from the boat. They were being hunted from below by some predator. Their situation was one of double jeopardy. Flying directly over the fish and following their progress, was a flock of sea birds that was sweeping down and snatching them out of the air each time they broke through the water. On a number of occasions after this event, we would find dead flying fish on the deck of the boat. I knew there were many species of flying fish and I had no idea what these were. They certainly were not big enough to eat as Joshua Slocum recounted in his book *Sailing Alone Around the World*, Chapter XII. He wrote, "Every morning except when the moon was large, I got a beautiful supply by merely picking them up from the lee scuppers." We did the same, but we just threw them overboard.

Because of the light conditions, I thought that British Bob might reappear over the horizon. The water being relatively flat, and the winds light, it was his kind of day. A catamaran is a very fast boat under the right conditions and I was sure, if he was heading for the Azores, that we would see him pass us. But no sail came in sight.

By mid-afternoon, the wind was still light so we lowered our sails and put up our colorful DRS again. We also dug the huge number one jenny out of its damp locker where we had put it a few days prior and hung it up behind the DRS to dry. When it had dried enough we folded it properly, and packed it again in the aft locker. Henk wisely suggested that we would do better to stick to the smaller jib for the rest of the trip. The conditions seemed to change so suddenly and with the difficulty of making sail changes, his suggestion to stick to the number two jib was well received.

WHEN CHECKING OUR FOOD inventory I noticed that some of the labels were coming off the cans. Thank God, we had packaged them in clusters in strong plastic bags, or we could have ended up with lots of *No Name* products and surprise dinners.

Unfortunately, we discovered that one of our two fresh water tanks was already empty. Henk began to wonder if his estimate of its capacity was exaggerated. We were not even halfway across to the Azores, and already one tank of fresh water was exhausted. We discussed getting the desalinator from the emergency pack and attempting to make more water with it. A reverse-osmosis desalinator makes seawater safe to drink by removing almost all of the salt. The one stored in our emergency kit was a hand-pump model that forced the seawater through a membrane. We still had a full tank of fresh water in the bow section, but we wanted to try out the fresh water device to see if it would work, and to determine what quantities it could produce.

Because the boat was much steadier, the work in the galley was easier. I was able to go back to the stove and stow the pressure-cooker under one of the bunks. But we were still in the Gulf Stream, and the cabin soon became unbearably hot. What a change! We went from extremes of temperature inside the cabin, just as we experienced extremes in the weather outside. With most of the hatch covers bolted down for the ocean crossing, it was difficult to get any cross ventilation. Up to now, it was impossible to open the large hatch over the main cabin because of the constant flow of water over the deck. For the first time we unbolted this hatch and let the cooler air flow through the cabin. It was a wonderful break for the cook.

It was so pleasant by mid-afternoon that I decided to try my hand at baking once again. I did a double batch of chocolate-drop cookies and they added a pleasant touch to our Beef Stroganoff that evening. While I was baking, Henk tried his hand at fishing. To me his bait looked like a large pink dildo. I wondered if he was after a mermaid. In any case, neither fish nor mermaid appeared on deck, much to my disappointment. A fresh fish dinner would have been the crowning cap to a wonderful sailing day.

When we were cleaning up after supper the wind started to freshen again. We had not changed the ship's clock since leaving Toronto so we were still operating on Toronto time and it was getting darker earlier each evening. As a result, shortly after supper we went on deck to remove the DRS and replaced it with the small working jib. We did not want to be on deck after dark. It was a good thing we moved quickly. The wind continued and by 1900 our time, it was clocking forty kilometers again, typical of sudden changes in weather. Henk's decision to go with the smaller jib was definitely a good one. We did not put up the main, and we were soon forced to reef the small jib as well. We wondered if the pleasant day of rest was the ocean's way of preparing us for what was to come.

I DREW THE MIDDLE watch, and it really was a black watch after the pleasant weather during the day. I went on deck dressed in my survival suit and I noticed how dark the night had become. There were a few breaks in the clouds and I did get a glimpse of the Big Dipper and part of the moon. "Hi, Maureen, I love you." The boat was tossing and turning once again, and I realized that the day before had been a welcome and rare rest from the constant pounding. I was glad to see the end of my watch two hours later, and to go below to the dry, warm comfort of the sleeping bag. The previous day's sun and calm sea had made the cabin dry again, and at least for the time being, it was a pleasant retreat from a long watch on deck.

Chapter 14

Because the day was June 8, our thoughts turned to our yacht club back in Toronto for it was Sail Past Day there. Sail Past is a tradition among yacht clubs, as it signals the official beginning of the sailing season. It is probably the one day in the year where the majority of club members sail together at the same time. The celebrations begin with a flag raising ceremony that pays tribute to the Canadian Flag, the American Flag, the Ontario Flag and the Club Burgee. A burgee is a triangular shaped pennant that has symbols or letters to identify the club and its location. At our club, the burgee is a dark blue background with gold symbols depicting the Scarborough Bluffs, and a spinnaker representing a sailing club. The yellow represents the sand of the bluffs, and the blue, the waters of Lake Ontario.

Following the flag raising ceremony there is a skippers meeting to outline the order of the sail past, and then all the boats head out on the lake. The commodore and flag officers of the club, usually dressed in white pants and blue blazers, are anchored in a fixed location. Each boat salutes the commodore as it sails past.

When all of the boats have returned to the dock, there is usually some sort of entertainment, followed by dinner and a dance. It is a day most members look forward to each spring, and for Peter, Henk and me, this is the first one we missed in fourteen years.

On the ocean, we were once again wrestling with strong winds, a topsy-turvy boat and a very reefed sail. The boat was moving at eight knots through the water. The sun had burst out but that had no effect on the waves. There was a commotion on deck as one huge wave crested beside the boat, and then dumped itself full force into the cockpit. The cockpit filled with water to the height of the seats, soaking the legs of the crew, before it was sucked clear through the scuppers. The boat did not slow down for a minute.

I again risked boiling water for coffee, having returned the Sea Cook to its place near the sink, and we enjoyed black bread, jam and cheese for breakfast. It tasted good even though it sounds like something fed to prisoners in solitary confinement. But in a sense, that was what we were—captives of our own dreams.

Henk, who was on the mid-morning watch asked me to get him a cold pop. Unfortunately, the supply I kept in the galley was exhausted and I had to go forward, screwdriver in hand, to remove some floorboards and get a new supply from the bilge where it was stored in plastic bags. Working on my knees, I was able to obtain a variety of pop cans, screw the boards back in place, and then work my way back to the galley section of the cabin.

When I thought I had figured out the motion of the boat, I let go with one hand in order to grab a new hold with the other. Clutching the plastic bag of pop, I stood up, let go of the edge of the bunk and reached for the handrail on the ceiling. Suddenly in the midst of this exchange, the boat made an unexpected lurch. Peter was asleep in the quarter berth at the time. I literally went off my feet, flew across the width of the boat, and landed on my head against the side of the hull just over the quarter berth. The bag of pop cans went flying somewhere and I landed unconscious on top of Peter, a large gash in my head. Peter woke up with a start and struggled to get out from under me, my blood flowing all over his yellow jacket. Henk screamed down the hatch to get me down on the deck. My unconscious state and the amount of blood flowing down over my face apparently threw a scare into the crew.

When I regained consciousness, Peter was sitting on the floor with my head resting on his lap. He was struggling with the first aid kit. I had noticed earlier that Henk had provided a very complete first aid kit, and on the advice of a doctor, he had included sutures and needles. My first thought as I regained consciousness was that Peter was going to sew up the wound on my head. The previous night Peter and I had sat together in that same spot. I held the mainsail on my lap and focused the flashlight on it while Peter sewed up a large rip. Now, I thought as I woke up, he was about to apply his skill to the top of my head. That image caused me to break out in laughter and Peter knew I was going to be all right. Henk told Peter to clean the wound and apply a bandage to stop the bleeding. Peter produced a purple colored adhesive one-inch square and quickly applied it to the top of my head. When I reached up to examine the damage, the bandage was neatly stuck to the top of my hair, a good distance from the actual wound. We both started laughing again.

After he cleaned the wound properly and stopped the bleeding, I got some wet paper towels to clean up the blood on my own face and clothes. There was really more blood than damage. I wanted to clean Peter's jacket as well, but he considered it a badge of honor, a symbol of our hardship. The blood did not disappear from his jacket until after many days of rain.

I REMEMBER READING ABOUT a sailor in the 1993 *Vendée Globe* single-handed round-the-world race. His boat was suddenly knocked flat on its side and the boom struck him on the head. He also was knocked unconscious in the cockpit. Unfortunately, he bit a large gash in his tongue and was forced to sew up the wound. Putting stitches in your own mouth, in the middle of the ocean, with the waves crashing down, must have been a terrible and painful experience. I figured I got off lucky.

Peter returned to his sleep and Henk got his can of pop. I was instructed to rest and, when Peter emerged from the quarter berth later, he was nice enough to prepare lunch for the crew.

I thought that we had encountered some large seas in the past week. But the conditions that afternoon defied description. The boat was being thrown around like a cork. One hand for self and one for the boat no longer applied. It was both hands for self! I felt as if I was in a bottle, and some giant was shaking it hard trying to get me out. There was an inferno of screeching wind and seas crashing on top of us. It was almost impossible to talk to each other. Swirling water cascaded in over the bulwarks and shook the whole boat the way a terrier might shake a rat in its mouth. We were now under a much-reduced jib, not much larger than a table napkin, and we were surging to twelve knots down the sides of the huge waves.

Inside the boat everything was in flux. The doors on the precious liquor cabinet on the right side of the companionway over the sink flew open, but miraculously the bottles landed safely in the quarter berth. Luckily, no one was trying to sleep there at the time. I got them back in their wooden holders and then tied the doors shut with a piece of leather line. What would Peter and I do without our daily shot of schnapps?

Attached to the upper part of the mast was a round metal radar reflector. Henk had put this up as an added precaution even though he had been told the aluminum steps that were attached to the mast were a better reflector for a ship's radar screen.

But if the truth be told, neither the small disc high on the spreader nor the aluminum steps on the mast are guaranteed protection from ships. That's why detection should not be left to such devices on a small boat. The two eyes of the deck watch are still the best protection, especially at night.

SHIPS USUALLY CARRY TWO kinds of Radar known as X-band and S-band. The X-band is good for detecting small targets like *RABASKA*. The problem is most ships do not use the X-band while at sea, only when the ship is near shore. The S-band, set at a 24-mile scale, is not sensitive to small targets and probably would not detect us even in normal conditions and probably not at all in a stormy sea.

Suddenly there was this loud crashing sound on the port side of the boat. When we checked, we discovered that the radar reflector had come loose and fallen into the water beside the boat. Because one line remained attached, it was being dragged in the water and doing its best to inflict scratches on *RABASKA*'s paint job. We recovered it quickly and stored it below.

In the midst of this chaos and excitement, I had to prepare dinner for the crew. The boat would ride up a wave, glide for a bit, before descending down the other side. If the wave was cresting the boat would ride it up, and just when it was going to go over the top, it would get smacked by the odd breaking wave. The cresting wave was forceful enough to knock the boat off course and cause the bow to yaw to starboard. It was a devil of a time adjusting the self-steering Monitor under those adverse conditions.

BECAUSE OF MY HEAD injury I wanted to go to bed early and get a good rest before having to take over another night watch. I climbed into the port berth, the only one with a lee cloth, and tried to sleep. It was impossible to lie on my side. The pounding of the boat over the waves would throw me up against the lee cloth and wake me up. If the lee cloth had not been there I would have been flung out of the berth and onto the floor repeatedly. Finally, I settled for squeezing my body somewhere between the bunk and the lee cloth. By lying on my back, I gained some stability and went to sleep with the help of a Tylenol for the headache. I am not sure my body slept, but the rest of me escaped from reality. Perhaps the bump on the head had some merit after all.

Much to my surprise I woke up at 0500. I climbed into my survival suit and went on deck. Henk was hunkered down on the low side of the boat well under the dodger. It was pouring rain and he looked exhausted. Peter and Henk had decided not to wake me during the night and each of them took an extra hour on watch. It was a miserable night for them but I was very thankful for their kindness and concern. When I realized what they did for me, I resolved to take a longer watch myself and let Peter, who would be following me on deck, catch up on his rest.

I was happy to meet the morning light and was rewarded with one of the biggest and most beautiful rainbows I have ever seen. What was even more fascinating with nothing to obstruct the arch, it was possible to see the complete rainbow from one end to the other. It was like a multicolored handle on the ocean and I wanted to reach out and lift the lid to see what was underneath. Perhaps after all there just might be a pot of gold or at least a pot of goldfish.

There were still many rainsqualls around but when the boat surged through the sunny spots, it was like going from early spring to summer in a few minutes.

At about 1000 I spotted a freighter in the distance and when I informed the skipper, he immediately jumped out of his berth and picked up the radio. Our first attempts to contact the ship were unanswered. We suspected that no one was on the bridge. We were afraid he would soon be out of both sight and range. Finally, a voice came over our VHF loud and clear. After some short greetings, Henk requested a weather report. Henk then asked the captain if he would relay a message back to Toronto. He agreed and the message we suggested was that we were fine, in good health, and enjoying our summer cruise one thousand miles offshore! Ten minutes later the ship radioed back to inform us that the call had been completed successfully. The phone number we gave him was Peter's home number. We had arranged for Peter's wife to relay the message to our wives.

While we could still see the ship Henk asked one final favor; could the captain see us on his radar screen? The answer came back that he could not. We quickly got the reflector from below, and Henk climbed up the steps on the mast and bolted it to the spreader on the port side near its old location. The ship then confirmed that he had a small blip on his radar screen. This was a great relief because we thought we were covered even without the reflector. It was a comfort to have it back in place. So much for the mast-steps theory.

I thought that we were pushing our luck with the ship captain, but a few minutes later the captain of the vessel called us to chat, or gam. In the days of the whalers, the tedium of looking for whales was alleviated when another whaling ship was raised on the horizon. The two ships would then draw close to each other, hove-to, and have a visit. We did not follow that tradition for obvious reasons, but we did have a short conversation, or gam, before he went over the horizon. He told us his ship, the *DOR DE BRAZIL,* was a 16,000-ton tanker carrying orange juice. As the conversation continued, the captain recognized Henk's slight Dutch accent. Henk then told him we had a German-speaking crewmember on-board as well. The captain then asked if he could talk to Peter. In the course of their conversation, they discovered they were from the same area in Germany. What a small world on a very big ocean. They talked in their native dialect until the ship was almost out of sight.

All of this may seem dull and very ordinary to someone on the land. But to be so far at sea for so many days without seeing or hearing from anyone but each other, was an event to celebrate and it lifted our spirits immensely. When the ship disappeared over the horizon it was like losing a good friend, and our world was suddenly a very lonely place once again.

Later in the day the wind actually subsided. Henk reconsidered his previous decision and suggested it was time to replace the working jib with the larger #1. Because of the lighter air, the task was completed without incident, and the skipper went below to continue his off-watch rest.

PETER CAME ON DECK later that day when the wind was beginning to pick up once more. The weather situation was constantly changing.

One hour we made one decision only to reverse it an hour later. The #1 was becoming far too much sail once again. Because it was an old sail, it was showing the stress, even when reefed. Peter and I decided to take it down and not bother the skipper.

Together we went on deck, lifelines secure, and managed to wrestle the jib down and place it on the foredeck. We got it pushed into the sail bag and worked it back along the deck, returning it to the same stern locker. Then we dragged the smaller jib forward and while Peter fed it into the track on the forestay, I pulled on the halyard to get it up.

Suddenly we had a major problem. The jib would not hoist no matter how hard I pulled on the halyard. It would rise to a certain point each time and then refuse to budge. There were things about this boat that only Henk could solve, and I thought this might be one of them. So once again, we rousted Henk from off-watch rest to ask for an explanation. Meantime the wind was increasing and the deck work was becoming more dangerous by the minute.

Unfortunately, not even Henk could get the sail to go up. I crawled along the foredeck and took up a sitting position in the pulpit to get a good look at the forestay track. About twenty feet above my head there was a small burr, barely discernable to the naked eye. It was shaped in such a fashion that it permitted the old sail to come down, but it stopped the replacement sail from going up. Each time the sail was hoisted it would jam against this spot and increase the size of the burr, aggravating the situation. The harder we pulled on the halyard, the larger the jagged edge became.

All three of us were huddled on the deck taking the salt spray over our bodies. I was still hunkered in the pulpit. Henk and Peter were clinging to the base of the mast. We decided someone had to go up the forestay and repair the damage. The jib had been our most used sail. Without it, we would have had great difficulty sailing under those conditions.

I think Peter volunteered to go up the stay! I did not catch the conversation he and Henk were having in the howling wind. Henk went back to fetch the bosun's chair, a canvas seat that can be attached to a spare halyard, and used to hoist someone up the mast. Peter got into the chair and tied a long line to the ring on his harness. Henk led that line forward to me in the pulpit. Then using the winch, Henk began pulling, as Peter went hand-over-hand up the mast. By now, the boat was pitching wildly on the waves, and because we lacked the drive ordinarily provided by the jib, the mast was swaying back and forth as the boat went sideways on the swells. Not only was there the up and down motion of the boat but a side-to-side swing of the mast as well. That made the situation very dangerous. When Peter was pulled to a point opposite the burr, about a third of the way to the top, I pulled him free of the mast and forward to the forestay. Letting go of his hold on the mast, and hanging between the mast and forestay, he began to swing freely like a slow pendulum on a clock, out over the water, first to starboard and then to port. It was paramount that I pull on my line quickly so he could grab the forestay with his hands and prevent a collision and serious harm. At that height the swinging and swaying was much more pronounced. It took all of my strength to get him into a position where he could grab the stay. Once there he tried to hold on with his legs, wrapping them around the stay. I could see he was taking a terrible beating as his body rolled back and forth with each rise and fall of the boat. It was a very terrifying situation and I was concerned that Peter would be seriously hurt.

He had taken a small file up with him, and as his body swiveled from side-to-side, he began to file the burr. His body was rotating back and forth around the stay, and he had great difficulty applying the file to the troubling spot. No sooner would he begin his work than the forces would slam him up against the stay, or try to pull his legs free from his perch. Finally, he managed to get the file onto the burr and smooth it down. We figured he had only one chance at this and we hoped he would be successful. The look on his face spoke volumes about what he was feeling and how difficult it was for him just to hang on and complete the task.

When he gave the signal, I let out my line and once again, he hung free between the swaying mast and the forestay. The danger now was he might slam against the mast as the boat came up to meet him. Peter was able to grab a ladder rung, pull himself against the mast, then climb down as Henk let out the halyard. He immediately scrambled back to the safety of the cockpit without a word. Henk and I tried the jib again and to our delight, up went the sail. Peter had done it!

Henk and I went aft and reefed in the sail with the jib lines to adjust it to the conditions and we were underway once again.

Meantime Peter had untied the leather lines on the liquor cabinet door, and got out a bottle of schnapps. I could not let him drink alone and I joined him for a quick one. My heart was pounding and the liquor felt wonderful as it warmed my inner being. Since Henk refused to join us in this celebration, we both had another drink in his honor. Oh, the burdens of leadership.

Below deck as I was preparing some lunch I noticed a foul smell coming from the fridge. I decided to clean it up and tie one of the lids open to allow the fridge to air.

Up on deck Henk had retrieved the desalinator from the emergency bag and was attempting his first batch of fresh water. In order to use two hands he had to sit on the cockpit floor and brace himself with his legs as he pumped away. He found it took about four large pails of salt water to make one quart of fresh water. I tried his fresh water, and decided it would be fine if we were really stuck, but if there was better tasting water available, I would stick to it in the meantime.

Chapter 15

At 0240 we crossed the halfway mark to the Azores. There was only another thousand nautical miles to our first port of call.

I was now able to read when off watch, in spite of the boat's motion, so I managed to enjoy a few chapters before grabbing some sleep in preparation for my next turn on deck.

As I expected when I went on deck that night, it was terribly black. The boat was moving well under the reefed jib alone. After confirming the course with the previous watch, I checked the boat and wind speed.

The only incident on my watch was the difficulty I was having with the moon. Early in the watch, I spotted a white light on the port side. It resembled the lights we had encountered off New York, the bright lights on the stern of fishing boats, but we were now well over one thousand nautical miles from shore. Could there be fishing boats this far out? I was curious as to what it might be. To confuse me even more, a red light appeared off the starboard bow. This would be unusual on a fishing boat, not because they did not have colored running lights, but because at a distance they would be blocked out by the bright working lights. If indeed it was a red light, then it led me to believe that the boat was heading in the opposite direction from us. What was even more confusing was that the bright white light seemed to be ahead of the red light. The difficulty in the dark expanse of the ocean without any reference points was determining distance and direction. Were they big lights on a freighter off in the distance or smaller lights on a fishing boat in relatively close proximity? I was confused.

Suddenly the lights disappeared! Very soon afterwards another light appeared, this time a red light and directly in front of the boat. There were a few visible stars ahead, but they were a good distance above the horizon and this light was low on the water. It seemed very close to us. I could usually figure out what was happening but this time I decided I needed another opinion. I called down and got the skipper out of his berth. He came on deck immediately. He looked at the light and said he had a similar experience the night before. In his case, the red light turned out to be part of the moon not concealed by clouds. I apologized for getting him out of bed in the middle of the night, but he understood how difficult recognition could be, and how important it was not to be wrong.

I kept an eye on it for some time. Then suddenly it disappeared, only to reappear again, but this time much higher and closer. I thought for a moment Henk was wrong and a freighter was indeed bearing down on us in spite of the absence of a green light. Should I call the skipper again or take evasive action? But the clouds broke for a moment, and it became evident that the light was, after all, coming from the moon.

The moon was like a cut fingernail, with only one small tip of it showing though the clouds. It was red in color and very low on the horizon, so it appeared as a red light to me. The ship's light was a false alarm but it provided me with some very anxious moments. Because I had awakened the skipper earlier, I did not disturb him at the end of my watch, but let him sleep another hour before calling him for his own watch.

Perhaps my confusion regarding the lights was an indication that the strain of the voyage was beginning to take its toll. Those lights harkened back to my fear of being run down by a freighter.

Sailors throughout the ages have recorded what was perhaps the embodiment of their deepest desires or fears. Even Columbus in 1492 on his first voyage to America reported that he had seen three mermaids and other strange creatures. Perhaps the famous kraken was a giant squid or colossal octopus and the little *PINTA* was only sixty-feet in length.

Years later, in 1608, Henry Hudson, during his second attempt to find a northeast route to the spice markets of China, wrote in his log on June 15, "This morning, one of our companie looking over board saw a mermaid, and calling up some of the companie to see her, one more came up, and by that time shee was close to the ship's side, looking earnestly upon the men…" (Henry Hudson, Hudson's Second Voyage 1608:The Northeast Passage). His sailors would have been familiar with seals and walruses and would not have mistaken them for something else. No doubt, the physical and emotional deprivation of a voyage can trigger fantasies. This might be the explanation for my confusion around the strange lights that night on the dark sea.

I finally got below and was soon asleep, only to be awakened at 0500 unable to sleep because of the boat's motion. I got out of the berth and informed Peter, who was now on watch, that I was going to make some coffee. It was blowing hard again with a large following sea. I figured Peter could use some schnapps in his coffee as well and of course added a little to my own. I then got into my survival suit and went up on deck to share the watch with Peter and to enjoy our hot drinks together.

We talked about our experience so far and agreed that some of the things we do sailing on Lake Ontario make sense only there, but made no sense out on the ocean. While we were sharing these great insights, we noticed to our dismay that one of the lines running from the steering wheel to the wind vane on the Monitor was badly frayed. When the skipper appeared later, (perhaps he smelled the hot coffee) and heard the conversation, he and Peter began repairs on the lines. I took the wheel for the first time since leaving New York. With the self-steering, no one was needed to be on the helm much of the time. Having to take a turn at the wheel only convinced me of the tremendous value of the Monitor. No one should ever leave home without it. It was a difficult task keeping the boat on course and it would become very exhausting and very wet, if any one of us had to be there twenty-four hours a day.

The wind was up again and a good sea was coming down on us. We left Henk on deck and Peter and I went below to get breakfast. I made pancakes served with maple syrup, black bread, cheese and apple juice, and, of course, more coffee. Not bad, considering the conditions.

AFTER BREAKFAST PETER AND I tried to get some sleep. With the boat pounding more than ever, the water coming over the port side was finding its way in greater quantities into the cabin. You could actually see it shimmering down the inside of the hull and into the quarter berth. It got behind the electric control panel and dripped off the light fixture that shone on the chart table. The port side berth was also getting wet. The water seemed to migrate into the back cushion, and then into the bottom cushion as well. When anyone lay on the bunk, it soaked into their clothes. I first noticed this when I lay down for a rest and the water started dripping into my face. I tried getting into a large plastic bag, but the water even found its way into that. The noise of the water hitting the plastic was like some kind of ancient Chinese torture. And so began my practice of wearing my survival suit even to bed!

There was one dry berth left on the boat, and that is exactly where the skipper headed when he came below from his watch. Peter was on deck and I was sitting on the port side, trying to keep my balance and avoid the dripping water below.

In spite of this our mood was excellent. So far only one day, when we were all wet, unaccustomed to the constant rocking, and apparently making no progress, were our spirits low. Peter was consistently a marvel. Any complaint was answered by, "It could be worse." For him each problem was a challenge, demanding a solution and a sense of humor. He had the nerve to refer to my large white plastic bag, the one I was attempting to sleep in from time to time, as an elephant's condom. I don't know what that made me!

I SUPPOSE IT IS only natural for three men on a boat in the middle of nowhere to talk about sex. Not that we got involved in deep discussions about this topic, but it seemed to emerge frequently in a humorous context. For example, there were comments about seeing topless water skiers when the weather was extremely bad. Often when one crewmember was lying down in the quarter berth, we would shout down the companionway that a group of topless skiers had just gone by the stern of the boat. Or we said we were sorry we had to awaken him for his watch when he was probably having a very interesting dream. Imagine what Sigmund Freud would do with all of this!

Our discussions were quite innocent and no doubt part of the male bonding process that is common when men are engaged together in some exciting and dangerous pursuit. At least the humor kept us from getting on each other's nerves. There are so many stories of crew getting into squabbles and even fights over small issues. This never happened on our boat.

Looking back, I now realize the innocent banter and sexual innuendos were a result of our need to get relief, not necessarily sexual relief per se, but some kind of physical relief from the extreme living conditions. I did find myself, especially when the conditions were exceptionally bad, having sexual fantasies. Not only was there no privacy on-board

RABASKA, but I was also afraid that if I found a way to actualize my fantasy, I would become blind and grow hair on the palms of my hands! At least that is what I was told as a teenager. Miles out at sea in the confines of a small boat with no privacy, sexual fantasies were the only relief available. So our references to mermaids and skiing topless beauties were our substitute.

By mid-afternoon, we were still moving along at six knots under the reefed jib. I found it necessary to do some mopping-up in the cabin. The water was beginning to slosh around, making it impossible to keep our socks dry. Henk was very unhappy with the situation. The boat had been in the shop the previous winter to repair the leaking above the waterline, but this had obviously not solved the problem.

We could not pinpoint the area where the water was entering the boat, but we felt it was along the jib-sheet track on the deck, or the teak rail that ran along each side of the cabin. Both track and rail were bolted through the deck and it might have been possible that these bolts were not properly caulked. I argued that there were times we drove the boat too hard putting great strain on the chain-plates and aggravating the whole situation. In reality as we found out later, the water was seeping in along the seam where the deck was attached to the hull. This was caused by the twisting action when the boat drove over the large waves.

Toward dinner time, the skipper called below to tell us he had spotted a number of whales off the starboard bow. Peter was resting and I was just finishing the mopping-up process and thinking about the dinner menu. We both hurried on deck. There were a number of water spouts about two hundred yards away. At first we could see very little of the whales' bodies so we had no idea of their size. They did not seem to be interested in us, and after a while, Peter returned to his bunk and I to my dinner preparations.

Suddenly the skipper called again. About five feet away and running parallel to the boat was a large whale. His head came alongside as he approached us from the stern. He actually gave us the eye as he moved slowly ahead of us. By the time his head was past our bow, there was still no evidence of his tail. It was as if we had come alongside an enormous smooth rock in the water. It is said that whales can measure up to 100 feet in length and can weigh as much as 150 tons. It would have been easy to step across and stand on his massive back. Just as suddenly, another monster appeared on our port bow. They were behaving much like the dolphins, but this time we were all a little nervous. If the dolphins miscalculated, there would be little affect on them or us. But if the whales moved in too close they could easily do damage to the boat. What if one got mad at us or flipped his tail? Even worse, what if a male thought we were a female whale and decided to get playful? Melville wrote in his story of *Moby Dick* that no man "can feel stranger and stronger emotions than that man does, who for the first time finds himself pulling into the charmed, churned circle of the hunted sperm whale." Back in the 1800s charging whales could, and did sink ships. In fact, in Herman Melville's book a white sperm whale actually sank the *PEQUOD.*

I have seen movies and pictures of whales and even stood on the deck of a large ship off the coast of Newfoundland and viewed the whales from that safe perch. But to have these huge mammals so close to a small boat was very frightening. More whales arrived, and we soon counted over fifteen waterspouts moving through the water beside us. They stayed with us only five minutes before they left to go about their business. I would have been just as happy if they decided they had seen enough and never returned, for it was getting dark and whales do not have running lights.

I was told by an experienced blue water sailor that they are not dangerous if in a group. Whales are peaceful creatures. They were probably feeding and not interested in us other than being curious. If a male is alone and sleeping on top of the water and the sailboat hits him, there could be a real problem. Whales are mammals and do sleep, but because they have to control their breathing, unlike us who breathe spontaneously, only sleep lightly.

Because commercial whaling is supposed to have ceased around 1964, there are still blue whales and right whales in the North Atlantic. I have seen right whales off the coast of New Brunswick in the summer months, but I suspect this was a rare sighting of a pod of right whales, the largest animal ever to have existed.

We were excited and alarmed at the same time. We handled the tension in the usual way, making smart remarks about the whales. Even though the pod had left, the first whale continued along beside the boat. Henk kept telling me that he was a paid-up member of Greenpeace. He claimed to have a membership card below with his papers. For a moment, I almost believed what Henk was saying! Much to Peter's disgust, I suggested that we might appease the whale by offering him a Becker Burger. Shortly after this, Peter returned to his bunk and was soon snoring. Perhaps he was not dreaming of Becker Burgers but of topless water-skiers circulating around *RABASKA* in place of the whales. Happy dreams, Peter!

SUCH WAS THE PATTERN of our lives: the sameness, the vastness of the water, the elements, the routine and then suddenly some exciting moment that made it all worthwhile.

For some reason we still had not adjusted the ship's clock even though we had passed through two time zones. Between New York and Horta, in the Azores, there is a four-hour difference in local time. Because of this oversight, it began to get dark even before we ate dinner. What should have been a dog watch began in the dark of night.

As the sun set, the weather turned cold once again. The Gulf Stream was now behind us, and the cold temperature was there to remind us that we were, once more, battling the cold North Atlantic. Bundled up in my survival suit, my *house*, I climbed into the cold dark cockpit to begin my watch. For once, the stars were visible, and what a sight it was. As I gazed up into the sky, I realized how little I knew about them, except they made me feel very small and insignificant.

What a mystery to behold! There were no city lights, or bright ship's lights to dull this spectacular canopy. *RABASKA* was alone in the world, and the sky was ours to possess in all of its magnificence. Because we depended so much on satellites, I was hoping to see some of them pass over our head. But I did not know where to look, so I just stared at the glorious ceiling that completely covered our little world. At one moment, I found my right hand reaching slowly above my head as if I could caress and fondle the unspeakable number of small lights flickering above my head.

When Peter came on deck, I remained with him, unable to drag myself away from the beauty over our heads. Together, like two old philosophers, we explored the mystery of life. Surrounded as we were that evening with such magnitude, we could not help but ask ourselves questions about the origin of the human race, and how we fit into the vastness of the universe that blazed above us.

Such an existential moment prompted Peter to tell me more of his life's story: his youth as an apprentice in Germany; his coming to Canada; and the various jobs he had held. I learned how he first met his wife and how much he appreciated the opportunities he found in his adopted country.

In the middle of our discussion the Skipper, unable to sleep and probably disturbed by our profound polemics, came on deck. Because the wind had abated considerably again, even though the waves had kept up their incessant motion, he decided to run the motor to recharge the batteries. The noise broke the magic of the evening, but not for long. We were pulled back to reality when, after a few minutes, the motor sputtered and suddenly died. The overheating alarm began to sound. The engine was either not getting cooling water and had overheated, or it was low on oil. Henk thought it might be the latter. We decided to wait till morning to assess the damage. Peter took over the watch, Henk fell asleep in the cockpit, and I remained on deck, as the boat bobbed and swayed on the swells with little wind to drive us forward.

Finally, I saw no sense in maintaining the jib as it was simply flogging itself to death as the boat listed to port and then to starboard, back and forth. I furled it in and went below. I started the Force 10 heater in an attempt to dry out the cabin and make our surroundings a little more comfortable.

Because of our failure to adjust the ship's clock, I awoke at 0415 and it was already bright outside. There was no wind and Henk and Peter were working on the engine. They had discovered there was no water going through it to keep it from overheating. The water outlet was tucked away under the long counter-shaped stern and it was difficult to see the emission. It was necessary to go aft and lean over the side of the boat to check the discharge. They would never have been able to find it in the night.

Working on the cabin floor as the boat bobbed on the windless sea, they soon learned that the impeller, a rubber propeller-like blade, was broken. It was easily accessible on the front of the motor. The companionway stairs had been removed and put on a bunk. The tools kept rolling out of reach, and the engine parts had to be carefully kept in a pot, stolen from my galley. My two crewmates asked me to keep watch on deck while they decided what to do next.

There were plenty of spare parts carefully stowed under the quarter berth. To replace the impeller was not a problem. But when the impeller was replaced, the pump simply did not pump water.

It became necessary to remove all the water hoses from the sinks and engine. Henk traced each line individually. They functioned as they should. What was the problem? Finally, a water pump inside the engine was taken apart and there they discovered the damage. A nylon ring that drove that impeller was seriously damaged. Although we had many spare parts on-board, we did not have that particular part. It was considered to be the one that *never breaks*. Here we were in the middle of the Atlantic Ocean with no wind and no engine.

Peter, ever the optimist, said every problem had a solution. He suggested we put our collective heads together and solve this particular one. After all, if we were able to solve the mysteries of the universe the night before, surely we could find a simple solution to our engine problem. I was on deck keeping watch and peering down into the cabin below from time to time to assess the progress of the two mechanics. Not knowing much about engines, I kept quiet. Peter discovered that a cotter pin was missing and unaccounted for. It appeared that it had never been installed or it had disappeared through the water system. He suggested making a pin from a bolt. We had plenty of spare bolts and nuts as well and Peter began to fashion one into a cotter pin using a hacksaw and a file. When he was ready and the motor was put back together again, I started it and the water flew out the stern pipe. They had done it again, or so I thought.

We all realized it was a very temporary arrangement and that we would only use the engine when absolutely necessary to boost the batteries. We needed nightlights and a working GPS to get us to Horta in the Azores.

After the cabin was restored to normal, we all went on deck to enjoy the noonday sun. We stripped off our dirty clothes at this second opportunity to take a cleansing bath. Thousands of jellyfish surrounded the boat. In spite of the proximity of large jellyfish, Henk dove overboard into an area where there were no jellyfish. Peter and I were more cautious and content to splash ourselves with buckets of cold salt water.

The Portuguese man-of-war swarming on the surface of the water around us had an inflated brightly colored bladder that was like a transparent sail. Actually, each man-of-war is a colony of specialized cells, or polyps that have tentacles that in some cases extend a hundred feet into the water. These tentacles have thousands of poison-secreting cells that are about 75 percent as powerful as cobra venom. Henk made sure none were near the spot where he chose to swim.

After our bathing, we had a leisurely breakfast before going back on deck. It was a relaxing moment, and even though the problem with the engine was frustrating, we enjoyed this respite from working the boat.

By mid-afternoon we were barely limping along. With all the portholes now open again and the center hatch thrown wide, the boat had a chance to air and dry out. It also smelled a little better, come to think of it!

At this time, I also decided to do something different and boiled a pot of tea. We had tea, black bread and canned oysters on the deck—all very proper. We wondered where British Bob was at the moment. Perhaps he was also enjoying a hot cuppa on his back deck as well.

We had a light supper and, those not on watch turned into their bunks early.

It was a terrible dark night and the beautiful stars were no longer visible. To make matters worse the wind was beginning to increase each hour. Because of our engine problems, the skipper decided not to turn on the riding lights. Naturally, this did not sit well with me, but I said nothing. We had very little defense against the freighters as it was, and to reduce what little we had, I thought, was reckless. I did a more intense lookout during my watch and hoped the others did the same while I slept. I also made good use of the flashlight shining it on the sail every fifteen minutes.

Finally I was relieved of my watch and went below. The wind continued to increase through the night and when I came on deck in the early morning, it was already a Force #6 on the Beaufort Scale or about 25 knots. The boat was soon back to its usual rock and roll motion.

Normally even when it was miserable on watch with the rain and the waves breaking over the quarter, we knew there waited a nice warm bunk below. We no longer had that luxury. The starboard lower bunk never fully dried out. We even tried pulling the cushion away from the cabin bulkhead to no avail. When everything else in the boat was wet, the moisture migrated very quickly. I kept my sleeping bag wrapped in a green garbage bag, but it seemed to pick up the moisture when in use. Crew coming below with wet clothing exacerbated the situation even though we tried to confine wet gear to the galley area.

When the cabin light came on during my watch, I knew someone was getting ready to relieve me. As delightful as that was, I also knew there was little to look forward to below deck—no warm and dry bed to welcome me. I tried to bed down without my survival suit and I simply struggled out of my *house*, hung it on one of the inside handrails to drip and slid into a very damp sleeping bag. It was not the reward I required after what always seemed like a long time on deck alone.

The next morning Peter decided that the repairs made to the water pump could be improved upon. He, like the rest of us, was not happy sailing at night without proper lights. He asked the skipper to dismantle the impeller housing once more in order to remove the broken cog. He worked for two hours on the cabin floor making a new cotter pin and gluing it into place. The skipper was very disappointed that the new engine he had recently installed had such an internal problem. He was led to believe, as we all were, that it was in good working order and that RABASKA carried all the extra parts necessary to make ordinary repairs.

The problems with the engine, coupled with the environment in which we were once again living, led to a deeper discussion around the problem of evil, not unlike the discussion found in the Book of Job—how to reconcile the existence of evil and suffering in the world with the existence of God. Henk wanted to know why all the bad things had to happen to him. Other boaters had their engines for twenty-five years and never experienced serious problems. Why him and why his boat in the middle of the ocean? Job denied the Old Testament mentality that misfortune is the result of sin, and like Job we tried to convince Henk that bad things happen to everyone and that he was not being centered out for special treatment.

Peter thought it a good idea not to prolong the discussion on the cause of evil and suffering, and sensing the potential tension, switched the conversation to our yacht club politics. Henk hinted that he thought he would run again for commodore. He felt the club was moving away from its original concept. Peter talked about some of the characters in the club, and before long we were all laughing, the problem of good and evil forgotten.

During the morning navigation session, Peter reported that we had only 688 nautical miles to go to our first stop in the Azores. Although we traveled a mere 88 nautical miles the previous day, we knew the current conditions would make up for lost time.

ONCE AGAIN, THE WIND and the waves were steadily increasing and the barometer was dropping rapidly. We thought a good hot breakfast would be in order to fortify us for the challenges ahead. My efforts to make pancakes were only partially successful. The boat was seesawing and when I put a spoonful of mix in the frying pan, it tended to run back and forth on top, while the bottom portion would stick to the pan. The result was that they tasted good, at least the cooked parts, but they did not look much like pancakes. By the end of breakfast, I learned to make silver dollar size pancakes.

For lunch we had the famous Macaroni Dinner. The only problem with this gourmet delight was that the instructions called for five cups of water—a rather extravagant use of our limited supply. It was also very dangerous trying to keep the precious water in the pot as it was boiling.

By late afternoon another severe storm engulfed us. We entered a sea where no laws prevailed, and we were forced below—no longer masters of *RABASKA*.

Chapter 16

It was the longest and most godless night of the trip. In late afternoon, the sea was getting very angry with us. The Beaufort was reading between Force #9 and Force #10, or winds of approximately 45 knots. Beaufort describes this as "a severe gale with high waves. Dense streaks of foam along the direction of the wind. Crests of waves begin to topple, tumble and roll over. Spray may affect visibility." The waves were beginning to reach twenty feet and dense streaks of foam danced on the water. The weather was cold and overcast. Every few minutes an occasional wave would crest over the stern of the boat dumping its load of briny froth into the cockpit, filling it to the top of the compartment seats, before being sucked out through the scuppers. We installed the heavy wooden panels in the companionway and locked them shut with cotter pins. If the boat rolled over too far, or one of the stern waves crashed against the companionway boards, we did not want them to be shattered. We had to make the boat as storm proof as possible. No large amount of water could be permitted to find its way below.

There was no shelter from the weather on deck. The boat would ride to the top of a wave, and, if the wave was not cresting, the boat would slither down the other side, often surpassing twelve knots of speed. There was a great sound of splashing as water and boat collided. Frothy spray flew in every direction and our fragile canvas dodger provided very little protection. We needed both hands to stay on the boat. I did not relish the idea of being washed over and dragged along the side of the boat attached to a tether. I knew I would never get back on-board. A camera shot would have told the whole story. Three men, dressed in foul-weather gear, gleaming from the salt spray, huddled together in the confined space of the dodger, clinging for dear life to the stainless steel binnacle stand. As the boat rose and fell, the three bodies were first compressed together in one direction and then thrust in the other, like three drunks sitting together in the back of a moving city bus.

Before complete darkness had descended on us, we realized we had to chance a few minutes on deck to reduce the size of the jib. When we were done, our only canvas was less than a foot square. It resembled a small white handkerchief clinging to the forestay, and leading us into the waiting storm. Earlier in the evening, I had prepared some sandwiches of very dry bread, canned luncheon meat and mustard.

We were finally forced to abandon the deck and went below, securing the hatch cover and the panels in the companionway behind us. We knew that by relinquishing the deck to the elements alone, there would no longer be any vigilance to see us through the night. Nevertheless, there was nothing we could do about it. To leave someone there would expose that crewmember to the danger of being washed overboard. We left the tiny bit of sail to keep us moving forward and prayed the self-steering Monitor would hold up against the mighty power of the waves. If the steering were to break, we would have to return to the deck and following the example of British Bob, put out a sea anchor and ride out the storm.

We crouched below in the dank, dark cabin eating our meager sandwiches. Henk ate part of his but Peter put his away for later and took a seasick pill. I ate mine, choking it down with a box of fruit juice and prepared myself to wait out the thundering storm.

Total darkness came upon us and the conditions continued to worsen. Our conversation turned to our situation. It was at this point that our diverse philosophies emerged. Although we knew the North Atlantic was unpredictable at any time of the year, our research had shown us that we were crossing during the most favorable time. Obviously, the weather was not cooperating with the statistical evidence! Henk wanted to keep the boat driving in order to move closer to our destination. Peter and I no longer cared about the destination or the course for that matter. Our concern was to keep the boat afloat. We felt safety of the vessel and crew were now of paramount importance. After considering all the possibilities, we finally agreed that when the storm abated, we could adjust the course and perhaps, even attempt to make up any lost distance.

Meanwhile things below deck were almost out of control. The one semi-dry berth on the starboard side was now out of the question. It would be impossible to stay in it for more than a minute. Even though the port berth was very wet, I climbed in, wet survival suit and all, and positioned myself between the bunk pads. Peter and Henk spread the cockpit cushions on the sole of the cabin, and hunkered down there to ride out the storm.

It was the longest night of the trip. The wind created a mournful howling sound as it traveled through the boat's rigging above our heads. Everything was rolling around. I could hear the dishes sliding back and forth and I waited for them to break free and come down on top of us. The canned goods, even the ones tied up in the garbage bags, managed to clatter against each other. The mast had discovered new ways to annoy us with its screeches and squeals. The gimballed stove broke loose from its pin lock and swung so far it crashed constantly against the side of the hull. The tools in their metal boxes were rattling as if someone had picked them up and was vigorously shaking them. The hull was groaning and creaking as it fought to move forward against almost impossible odds. Everything below deck including the crew was in a state of constant motion.

When a tenth wave burst against the port quarter, the sound was deafening. It was as if some colossal monster was smacking us with a telephone pole. Each explosion was followed by tons of water cascading over the coach-house roof, slamming into the dodger, and rushing into the cockpit before escaping over the stern and through the scuppers.

It is hard to believe, but in the midst of this wild cacophony, all three of us finally went to sleep—not because we were relaxed or unafraid, but simply because we were totally exhausted.

Chapter 17

DAWN WAS BREAKING WHEN I awoke. Peter and Henk were still slumbering, their bodies slipping and sliding, back and forth, across the cabin floor. The inside of the boat was less deafening and much of the noise had abated. I realized the storm was over.

The first thing I did was locate a camera and take a picture of the inside of the boat and the two sleeping beauties on the floor. Next I put on the kettle to make coffee. Then I decided to finally abandon Toronto time and try to figure what time zone we were actually in. I thought the best idea was to set the ship's clock for Greenwich Mean Time. I moved the clock hands from 0750 to 1150. It was time to wake up the rest of the crew and ask them how they enjoyed their extra four-hour sleep-in!

During the morning the wind and waves continued to abate. The steering vane held through the storm and we were close to our course. By mid-morning the wind was down to 15 knots and coming in from the north. It was cold as we reset the jib and moved the boat closer to the rhumb line. A simple definition of the rhumb line is what you get when you draw a straight line between two points on a chart. Of course, when you are sailing transatlantic, it was important to remember that the shortest distance between two points is not always a straight line. So getting knocked a bit off course on the chart's rhumb line is not a matter of major concern.

During the day we took turns on deck, but the rest of the day was spent sleeping and regaining our strength after a very stressful night. For dinner that evening, we had penne, made with homemade sauce, all of the sauce ingredients, except the garlic, from a can. Unfortunately, penne tends to slide around on a flat plate. Henk, sitting in the cockpit with the plate on his lap, had no sooner taken his first bite, than the boat lurched and he was wearing half of his dinner. What was missing was some kind of large bowl that could replace the plates. I resolved I would look for something at the first opportunity. I did not like my painstakingly prepared dinner ending up as a jacket decoration.

The crew seemed to adjust to the time change. Peter continued to do the navigation, using the GPS and double-checking our progress on the chart. The skipper would check the calculations as a double precaution. Every day, or once in each twenty-four hours, Peter would plot our progress on the paper chart. This way I could go below and see how far we had traveled, check the distance to go, and calculate the number of days remaining at sea.

The conditions were wearing us down but Peter was always ready with a comment that would make us laugh again. Once the skipper asked Peter to provide some information about our course. Peter was taking some time doing the calculations. Henk was anxious to know whether it was necessary to adjust the steering Monitor. After a few minutes, he asked Peter a second time for the information. Peter paused, put down the dividers he was using to measure the distance on the chart, moved to the companionway, looked up at Henk and said, "If I get it right the first time will you give me a kiss?" We all burst out laughing.

That evening after supper, I was sitting on deck with the skipper, the time change having given us longer evenings with sunlight. I mentioned that the white caps gave the appearance that the waves were breaking on rocks. I knew ocean swells began to curl as the water got shallow, and then crashed onto the sandy beach or rocky coast. It was a new experience for me to see these waves doing the same thing, but in the middle of the ocean on top of each other. To me it looked like they were breaking over a shoal, even though we were still hundreds of miles from the nearest shore. I was immediately informed that there were no rocks in the vicinity. I was not sure he understood my comment so I let it pass.

The part of the engine that Peter repaired with glue the previous day was left to dry overnight and then replaced in the engine. Everything seemed to work well, but we decided to save the engine for docking when we arrived in the Azores.

Henk had the first black watch that night. As the sun set it became evident that we could expect another cold night. I put the usual plastic box of goodies under the dodger on the coach-house roof. It consisted of some chocolate bars, fruit drinks, nuts and dried fruit. On examination each morning the box was always empty. That night I knew I had the 0100 to 0300 watch and then the 0700 to 0900 watch so that meant only one black watch or night watch. I don't think I could have taken another night like the previous one.

At 0045 I was awakened with a flashlight shining in my eyes. This was a hint from the deck that I was due for my watch. Past experience had taught both Peter and Henk that I needed about fifteen minutes to struggle into my *house* and get dressed for the watch. So I rolled out of my cozy, but still damp sleeping bag, and began the struggle into the survival suit. I had anticipated that the suit would only be necessary for the first week out of New York, and then it would be shorts and T-shirts. But at that point in our voyage, we had only had two warm days and that was during our time in the Gulf Stream. There was still a long way to go, and time to enjoy a summer cruise, or so I had hoped.

When I first went on deck, the wind was still coming in from the north. The waves were fifteen feet high. Every now and then, they would break over the stern quarter and spray the cockpit, so I was happy to be bundled up in my suit. We passed through a few rain showers that added to my discomfort. Later that night the sky cleared and once again, I was comforted by the magnificence of the starry dome above us.

Because my watch strap had broken the day of the storm, I had no way of telling when to get the next deck watch up for duty. I did not want to be shining the light down the hatch every twenty minutes to look at the ship's clock. I felt that would indicate to the resting crew that I was anxious to get below as soon as possible—which I was of course. So I kept awake by adjusting the wind vane, gazing at the sky, and wondering about the gigantic expanse of water know as the North Atlantic Ocean. Neither ever seemed to end. Although every day was different, every day was the same. As Peter would say, "You can't see the waves for the waves."

My watch passed slowly and when I slid the hatch cover open and shone the light on the clock, to my amazement it was 0345! The first week it was not necessary to wake each other for the night watches. But as we had become accustomed to life on-board, it was easy to sleep beyond the four hours. I had been on deck two hours and forty-five minutes. I shone the light on Peter, just as the skipper had shone the light on me. Fifteen minutes later Peter appeared on deck dressed in his usual wet gear.

Peter had brought along a cotton cowl type headpiece that pulled down around his neck and shoulders. We referred to it as his Mother Teresa hat. It was light blue in color and made a perfect frame for his white bearded face, giving him a cherub-like appearance. When he first put his head through the companionway, I was always reminded of a Michelangelo fresco in the Sistine Chapel. Over the top of his cowl, he tightly secured the hood of his wet weather jacket. I don't think the arrangement kept Peter dry or warm, but he did not complain.

I retired below to my bunk and was soon asleep. I was awakened by the ship's clock striking seven bells. I was late for my second watch and no one had called me. It was important to all of us that we do our share on deck. I felt that if I was late I was letting someone down. So I quickly got into my suit and climbed on deck. Henk informed me that he had only been there one hour! The deck watches had been pushed back one hour because I did not want to be constantly shining the light below. Henk asked for a cup of coffee, which was just what I needed as well, for things were still wet, cold and miserable.

Because the Sea Cook was gimballed in four different directions, it was much more reliable than the stove. I gave up on the stove a couple of times as it only swung up and down and not sideways. As a result, heating water tended to slosh back and forth until it finally jumped out of the pot. I had to use a pot, because during one particular bad day, when the boat made a sudden lurch, I knocked the kettle onto the floor. To make matters worse, I lost my balance at the same time and stepped on it. Not only did I flatten part of it, but also it leaked where the handle had been torn loose. Hence I had to boil coffee water in an open pot on the Sea Cook. If I wanted to remain healthy, the pot demanded constant attention.

Holding on with one hand, I had then to get the boiling water, instant coffee, canned milk and sugar into the cup without spilling too much on the sole. The next move was to pass it up through the hatch without falling over on whoever was asleep in the quarter berth. This was always a dangerous move, and holding onto the boat and transporting a hot cup of coffee, was a constant challenge.

During the course of our journey, we had succeeded in demolishing most of our coffee cups. Of the two or three that were left, only one had a handle. I had brought along an L.L.Bean thermos cup with a lid. Not only did it keep the coffee or soup hot, it also prevented it from spilling. I discovered on a few occasions, it could even bounce along the deck without breaking. More thermos cups would have been useful, especially for safely transporting drinks to the deck.

Henk and I sat together under the dodger and sipped the hot coffee. Suddenly, directly in our wake, there arose out of the water the enormous broad back of another whale. He was alone and he confirmed his presence with a large plume of water. I have no idea why I assumed the whale was a he, perhaps it was because it was alone. As he glided quietly behind us, he resembled a two-lane highway, the backbone like the line down the middle of the road. Henk went for his camera but Peter refused to get out of his bunk.

One part of me wanted the whale to be there, but another part wanted him to leave. It was so big, and we were so small. What if we slid down a wave and accidentally bumped into the whale? What would happen? Why was he following us in the first place? He swam quietly in our wake for a long time and then, just as suddenly, he dove below us and was gone.

While Henk and I were keeping an eye on the whale, Peter got breakfast. He cooked scrambled eggs and fried potatoes. We were out of fresh bread and given our circumstance, it was impossible to bake new loaves as I had planned.

We continued to sail at six knots with the jib alone for the rest of the day. We figured we could average about one hundred miles in a twenty-four hour period. It being a Friday, we had hoped to reach the Azores early the following week.

Chapter 18

THERE WAS NOTHING BUT endless water all around us. The visibility was excellent for about twenty miles in all directions. But there was nothing to see but water. I began to wonder if there really was land out there somewhere.

The weather cleared that day toward noon and the sun appeared, but with the north wind, it remained very cold. I went below for a siesta after lunch. Because the boat was wet inside and my berth very damp, I followed Peter's example and slept on the floor of the cabin.

When I returned on deck, we were sailing east so the sun was directly behind us. By keeping low under the dodger, it was possible to feel the sun's warmth. I returned below and dragged a bunk cushion on deck making sure to protect it from the spray. The covering dried quickly but the sponge-like interior remained wet. As soon as I applied any pressure to the cushion, the fabric was immediately soppy again. My efforts were in vain, for as soon as I returned the cushion to the bunk below, nothing had changed.

At 1730 we spotted a freighter on the starboard bow. This was the first one we had seen since the previous Sunday. It was evident that his course would take him in front of us, so we decided to call him when he got closer. The skipper was on our radio for fifteen minutes before his call was returned. Again, I suspect no one was on deck and the captain had to come from his cabin to answer the call. His English was good, but he had a pronounced Latin accent. Henk again requested a weather report and asked if a message could be sent to Canada. We were asked to stand-by on the radio. About twenty minutes later the ship called us and asked about the message. Henk repeated his request, and once again, we were asked to stand-by. We waited and watched as the ship slowly disappeared over the horizon never to be heard from again! How different this was from our first experience with a freighter.

During our wait for the reply that never came, we were entertained by a school of dolphins. They were much smaller than the ones we had encountered before, but they were just as playful and it was as if they were trying to console us when the ship failed to keep up communication.

Other than that incident, the day went well and we managed to track one hundred and thirty nautical miles in the twenty-four-hour period. The wind shifted to the north and blowing well, made us feel that the four hundred miles ahead of us no longer seemed like a long way. We were getting anxious to reach land, to stand still and to dry out.

I DREW THE MID watch and it was a very black night. I felt very lonely and was anxious to smell land. Halfway through my watch, I was visited by my friends the dolphins. I needed to see them badly, and as if they were aware of my need to be with Maureen, they had come to console me. There were eight of them and they put on a special show. Usually you just see their back out of the water for a moment as they breathe, but this time as they sped through the water, they jumped clear of the surface and flew through the air. What was even more impressive, they did it in unison, as if they had been trained in some marineland. They were perfectly choreographed again as if moving on a given signal. Finally, they went to the bow of the boat for their usual frolic, and then disappeared into the night. What fun it was to watch them and how thankful I was for their visit.

At the end of my second watch, I kept sweeping the surface of the water looking to see if the whale was following in our wake. Again, I was disappointed he was not there, but relieved at the same time. I went below and made coffee before awakening Peter for his watch. I then went to the side of his bunk and offered him coffee in bed. He refused, but said he would join me on deck as soon as he got into his wet gear. A few minutes later I realized why he did not want his coffee in bed. On his way past the liquor cabinet, I saw him add a daub of vodka to his cup. I lowered my cup through the hatch for a bit of the same.

Later I prepared a breakfast of eggs, canned corn and bully beef. When Henk smelled the food, he joined us for breakfast. While I cleaned up Peter and Henk again worked on the navigation. The time had come to get more serious, and to start working with charts that were more detailed than the large ocean chart we had been using up to that point. The problem of working with the new chart was the distances now appeared much longer on that new scale. What looked insignificant on the large chart looked overwhelming on the small one.

Early in the trip, Henk had graciously offered to do the dishes at the end of each day. This was a great relief for the cook, and also provided a great source of entertainment. First, I would get all the pots and dishes together and hand them up to Peter. Meanwhile, Henk would retrieve a large pail of seawater from the ocean. Using Sunlight soap and a scouring pad, he would wash the dishes in the soapy water. He then dumped that over and refilled the pail with clean water for a rinse. Situated between the skipper and me, Peter would dry the dishes and hand them back to me for storage.

However, what was most entertaining were the conditions under which Henk had to do the dishes. He would sit on the floor of the cockpit, dressed in his storm suit, and brace the pail of water between his legs which were pushed up against the side of the boat. Then using both hands, he would begin to wash the dishes. Most of the time the water would be spraying over the port quarter giving Henk a wash of his own.

On a number of occasions, he took the full brunt of a cresting wave. Naturally, the dishes that were waiting to be washed slithered around the deck and even flew the full length of the cockpit. This explains how so many coffee mugs were broken, and why the remaining few had lost their handles. We also lost some cutlery that had found its way down the scuppers when a wave crashed over. In spite of these challenging circumstances, Henk was most faithful in performing this humble task every evening. It should be pointed out however, that dishes washed in salt water don't really dry well, and were usually put back in the cupboard damp and salty.

As we drew closer to land, the time dragged on and on. Although the boat was moving forward, there was no sense of gaining ground. We were in the middle of the large black vinyl record, surrounded only by its edge. We kept saying we would see land in four or five days. But those days passed, and no land came in sight.

I WAS ON THE first watch of the evening. That meant I would get another black watch at 0400. I call this arrangement the double black, after the signs you find on the ski hills. Double black diamonds mean steep and dangerous hills. And we were finding a lot of steep and dangerous hills on the ocean.

During the night, the wind dropped even further but the waves continued to rock and shake the boat. The only way I could get the boat to move forward was to disconnect the self-steering and take hold of the wheel myself. It was also necessary to fall about thirty degrees off course if I wanted to get any boat momentum.

Prior to my going below after my first watch, I had spotted a light on the starboard side. Since it was a very bright stationary light, I concluded it was a fishing boat. Probably one Brian Tobin had chased from the Grand Banks a few years ago. I did not want to get too close in case he spotted our Canadian flag.

When I returned to the deck later for my second night watch, the wind had picked up considerably. Both crew on watch had hand-steered the boat off course as I had done. However before Peter went below, we thought we could reset the self-steering Monitor and readjust the sail as the conditions were becoming more favorable. I did not relish another two hours staring at the compass light. Soon the boat was tracking eight knots and we were slicing through the chop and waves on our way to land. The wind continued to increase and it was necessary to shorten the jib sail once again. It was not long before the Beaufort scale registered between Force #8 and Force #9, or over 40 knots, close to 50 miles per hour. And, of course along with the wind came the rain and big waves. It appeared we were in for yet another major storm. It was difficult to stay on deck and all three of us, with our safety lines securely attached, hung on for dear life. We huddled together like three drowned rats, or the three stooges, under the dodger. It was impossible to keep dry. Below decks once again had become a disaster area. Whatever was not tightly secured was banging and clanking. When I went below I tried to write, but I doubt if I would have been able to read my own writing afterwards.

The skipper had suggested that we take off our wet gear in the galley area to keep some of the water out of the rest of the boat. Unfortunately, the galley section was the most dangerous part of the cabin. The handrails along the inside of the coach-house roof did not extend over the galley section. There was very little to hold on to, so getting in and out of our wet gear was very difficult. The shield that was intended to protect the quarter berth from spray, also had a small handhold. But it had been literally destroyed by the skipper one day when he lost his balance and went flying across the galley and smashed into it.

To get out of our wet gear the only reasonable choice was to sit down on the berth or on the floor. We tried to perform this chore in the galley area, but most of the time we ended up on the berth anyway. We also wanted to hang our gear on the handrail to drip dry. If the boat remained upright the gear would drip on the floor. But most of the time they just swung back and forth, dripping on both berths. So even if it was possible to change in the galley, the water ended up on the bunks anyway. Henk and I began to sleep more and more without even removing our suits. At least they were dry inside.

During the day, another huge freighter appeared on our starboard side. We saw him in plenty of time and knew there was no danger, but we did not see him come up over the horizon. By the time someone saw the ship, he was steaming along our starboard quarter. Once again, Henk called the freighter and asked for a weather report. It was read in monotonous English that suggested it meant nothing to the reader. As a result, we did not understand most of it. The ship assured us we were visible on his radar, and then he slipped into the mist and rain, disappearing as suddenly as he had come.

Henk figured it was again a good time to start the cabin heater. He knew it was impossible to dry things out, but at least it would warm the place up and make it livable. Even the cabin heater was showing the strain. The exhaust pipe that extended up through the coach-house roof was now brown with rust and covered with dry salt. It had been a pretty heater, but it now looked like something you would find at the city dump.

Chapter 19

Aʙᴏᴜᴛ ᴛʜɪꜱ ᴛɪᴍᴇ, ᴀ very strange thing happened to all of us. At one point, I wanted to speak to Henk who was below hammering pegs into the mast collar. When I put my head through the hatch to call him, I could not think of his name! The only name that would come to mind was that of a friend and co-worker from many years ago. Instead of Henk, I called *George*. Henk was having a similar experience with me. Later that same day he called me *Bob*. At first I though he was teasing me because of my *faux pas* earlier. But he was having the same *lapsus memoriae*. Bob was an old time friend and co-worker of his. I wanted Henk's assurance that his old buddy was a good guy, especially if we were to keep up this behavior.

We both experienced this strange phenomenon for a couple of days. Meanwhile during the same period Peter started to sing a German rhyme over and over again. Whether he was on deck alone or somewhere in the cabin, you could hear Peter singing. All of us were moving back in time and we could not find an explanation for our strange behavior. No doubt the most likely explanation was fatigue and exhaustion, as none of us had yet reached the age of senility.

I must say that I was alarmed at this strange behavior. I knew somehow that it was related to quality sleep deprivation. It was impossible to get a good sleep because of the noise, the constant motion, the wet environment and the steady strain of managing our lives and the boat under the adverse conditions in which we were now living.

My concern was that fatigue could affect safety, impair performance, cause accidents and hurt our ability to concentrate. Fatigue would be the cause of nodding off when on night watch, slow reaction time and most of all it would result in poor decision-making.

That evening, I decided to try to get some sleep right after the dinner dishes were done. I lay down in the one remaining semi-dry berth, but the rocking was so bad I just kept falling out on the floor.

Before I knew it, I was called for my midnight watch again. Of course, it was drizzling on deck and the boat was pitching badly. I noticed our masthead light was burned out, and when I reached for the night snack-box it was gone, washed over by a wave slipping under the dodger. By 0200 when Peter came on deck to relieve me, I was ready to go below. I felt sorry for Peter having to come up on deck, but I felt worse for myself having to go to the wet mess below. I went down, flopped on the cabin sole and once more attempted to get some sleep.

When I returned to deck for my next watch at 0600 Henk was just sitting there in a daze, the rain coming down on him in buckets. He looked ready to quit. He was obviously very tired and run-down. I offered to get him a cup of coffee if he would stay on deck a few more minutes.

We were now keeping the water tank turned off to prevent loss through a leak in the system. We figured this was how we lost so much fresh water out of the first tank. The tap that controlled the water was located under the port berth. Peter had gone below exhausted and finding me asleep on the floor had dropped into the port berth and was asleep. I did not want to wake him to get to the tap, but I did find another way in and soon I had the water boiling for coffee.

Back on deck the wind had died again but the boat was rolling over to thirty degrees—first one way, then the other. I sat in the rain for two hours and watched man-of-war jellyfish that surrounded the boat. Some were very small, others quite large, and their colorful sails glistened in the mist. They raised what looked like a head, and put a twist in their sail. Like us, they too were looking for the wind.

It was demoralizing to be only few miles from our destination with no wind and no motor. If we were sure we could count on the motor to perform, then we would have motored to the harbor at Horta. Like ancient mariners, we had to sit and wait for wind. I cooked the last of our eggs for breakfast. Later the wind began to increase, and with it, our spirits. A light wind continued all afternoon and cleared the skies. Huddled under the dodger, the sun was warm. For the first time in a few days, I removed my survivor suit and enjoyed the pleasant and warm caress of the late afternoon sun. There was plenty of sea life around us. There were birds, man-of-war jellyfish, dolphins and two large turtles, their corrugated shells shining in the sun. Even a couple of whales sauntered by. It was like a military review of all forms of life we had encountered thus far on our journey. It was nice to have their company.

FOR DINNER THAT EVENING, we had salmon on rice, corn and green beans. All the ingredients were fresh out of a can, but it was wonderful how good it all tasted. Our appetites had been whetted by so much bad weather. A little spice also helped and Peter quietly watched me chop in fresh garlic and did not complain.

I spent the early evening below reading. I had brought along my own small reading lamp and extra dry cells, so that I would not be making a demand on the boat's power system. Given the problems with the motor, I was glad I brought the little lamp along.

I went on deck for my watch at 2200. The wind was light. Each time we glided up over a swell and started down the other side, the jib would lose its wind and make a loud slapping sound. A school of dolphins raced by but did not stop to play with us. I was disappointed.

I got to bed at midnight and was awakened by the ship's clock at 0430. I thought I had read the bells wrong, believing it could only be 0030 so I went back to sleep. I woke up again and this time checked the clock with my flash light. It was 0500 and I was an hour late for my watch. When I stuck my head out of the hatch to apologize, Henk said he was comfortable and decided to let me sleep. I climbed into my suit and decided to go on deck without my sea boots. This proved to be a big mistake because the rain started in earnest, and I spent the next three hours with very wet and very cold feet. I say the next three hours because I decided to let Peter sleep as well.

At dawn I spotted a fishing boat. The visibility was not good so I went below and turned on the VHF radio just in case the skipper of the fishing boat wanted to call us. However he did not move from his location, and we passed him by, leaving him far behind on our starboard side. A fishing boat was a good sign, as it meant we were getting closer to land.

Peter came on deck at 0800 thankful for the extra sleep. I went below and made coffee and came up on deck where Peter and I resumed talking about our experiences and our various jobs.

At 1000 Henk and Peter began to do some serious navigational work. We were definitely close to land and you could smell it in the air. They figured that we were sixty-two miles offshore, having traveled only twenty through the night. They hoped we would raise land before the end of the day. I could feel the excitement as the reality of land was a definite possibility. I went below and got out the navigational books to write up a description of the approach to the harbor at Horta.

The Azores are made up of nine islands. Two of the islands, Corvo and Plores, were further north than we wished to sail. Our destination was Horta, on the island of Faial. Horta is a famous stopping-off place for recreational sailors from all over the world. Some are returning from the Caribbean, others, like us coming from North America, and the majority arriving from Europe.

While they worked, I got breakfast. All the eggs were gone and I wanted to make a batch of pancakes. I read somewhere that a teaspoon of vinegar and soda, dissolved together, would replace one egg. Along with fried potatoes and brown beans in honey, I prepared black bread soaked in olive oil and balsamic vinegar. Not the kind of breakfast one might have on Sunday morning at home, but there were no complaints from the busy navigators.

As we approached Faial, the weather began to settle in once more. With frequent rainsqualls and the heavy clouds, the visibility was poor. By dusk, we were still twenty miles offshore and night was falling. We had to make a decision to attempt a landing or stay offshore till the morning light. We decided to take a chance on the weather clearing and try to reach port during the night. The charts indicated a well-marked harbor and we hoped it would be clear enough to see the lighthouses along the shore and the lights of the city of Horta.

There was a lot of chatter in Portuguese on the VHF radio. Although we could not understand a word, it was another assurance that we were approaching land.

No matter what happened, we knew it would be a long night. No one wanted to go below and sleep with the land so close. I still found myself doubting that land truly existed, but Peter assured me that it was really there somewhere in all that rain and mist.

For dinner, I cooked up vegetables and onions in the pressure cooker, accompanied by canned ham, mustard, garlic and honey. By 2000 we were still eight miles offshore and the weather was getting worse. The skipper was showing the stress. We all knew there was real danger. If for some reason we had miscalculated in our navigation, we could run up on the rocks in that poor visibility.

Peter, as usual, was ready to deal with the tension. Earlier in the trip during one of our discussions under the stars, he told me a story about an East Indian guide. The tourist guide was explaining to his group the important role elephants played in his country's history. In the course of his dialogue he noticed that one of the large elephants was about to void its bladder. So the guide turned to the tourists and said, "Now we come to the exciting moment when the elephant lets go of his water."

The poor visibility, the fine rain, and still no sign of a lighthouse led to an increase of tension. The skipper was not enjoying the moment and was concerned for our safety. With the possibility that the motor would not work, with no wind, and with the shore very close, Henk had good reason to be tense and to be verbally expressing his exasperation. I was working below making sure we had the right light sequence along the south shore of the island, and trying to locate a spot on the map where we might tie up for the night in the harbor.

Suddenly in the middle of the skipper's grumbling on deck, Peter, his Mother Teresa cap in place and water streaming down his gray beard, put his head down the hatch and said, "Now we come to the exciting moment when the elephant lets go of his water." We both burst out laughing. We were like little children on Christmas Eve, full of great expectations, and frustrated that things were not moving fast enough.

Finally, about 2100 I spotted a light on the port bow. Everyone strained their eyes to make sure that I was not seeing things. It was not long before the light was visible to all three of us. We knew where we were on the chart and the tension eased. Peter went below immediately to take a fix and estimate of our position based on the sighting of the lighthouse. Our chart indicated a permanent flashing light of increased brilliance situated on Castillo Branco Point.

We still had to sail ten miles down the coast in the drizzle and light wind, before we could make our turn into Horta harbor. We knew from our reading of the area that there was a large point jutting out into the ocean that partially hid the entrance and its lights. It was so black we could see nothing but the light itself.

Since Peter made his final repair on the engine, we had not started the motor, not even to charge our batteries. If his repair did not work, and the engine heated up, we would have great difficulty maneuvering into the port. Once in the harbor we could run the motor long enough to get tied up without doing it serious damage. We could not take the chance of having it fail offshore, depriving us of the docking advantage later. So we slowly sailed down the coast of Faial five miles offshore, until we reached the channel entrance between the islands of Faial and Pico. It was a very slow journey and we prayed the visibility did not get worse.

As we approached the channel, Monte da Guia loomed on our port bow. From our approach, the lights of Horta were divided by the huge volcanic rock formation. It made it very difficult to determine the actual entrance to the channel that separated the two islands. We carefully sailed well past the rock until we could see the green and red lights on the breakwater at Horta.

We hardened up onto a port tack and began our entrance into the channel. Suddenly the huge rock to port changed in appearance. Rather than a huge black blur blocking out the city lights, it turned an eerie gray and resembled an iceberg. Was British Bob right after all? Had we sailed too far north? As we drew closer, it became apparent that the rock formation had become enshrouded in thick fog. It was bizarre, as there was no sign of fog anywhere else. However, behind the fog formation the red and green lights on the breakwater were still clear. We steered for them leaving Monte da Guia on our port side. The wind was light and a strong tide was running out into the sea. Under jib alone, we made very slow progress.

I was sitting on the coach-house roof to get a better view of the harbor ahead of us. I looked back toward Monte da Guia and yelled to Henk to get a quick fix on the light at the end of the pier. One very black rainsquall was coming off the mountain and about to enshroud us in its thick mists. We needed a compass course because the little red light that was guiding us was about to disappear. Along with the fog, there came a very strong squall. It was a good thing we were sailing under jib alone.

We sailed another two hundred yards in a total blackout before the squall passed. It cleared just in time for us to see the end of the breakwater. We pulled into the harbor, took down the jib and tried the engine. It worked! But because the harbor was still in a deep mist and new to us, we had to find a dock quickly. We searched for a spot to tie up. To our surprise, the harbor was full of sailboats. Where did they all come from? The only boat we saw on the ocean the whole time was British Bob, yet every dock was rafted three and four deep.

Some good person on a large service barge suggested we cross over to the seawall and tie up on the inside of the breakwater till the morning. Using our searchlight we motored to the wall. The skipper was on the wheel and he skillfully maneuvered the boat into a spot between two other sailboats. When we were close enough, I scrambled up the wall onto the dock with the stern line of *RABASKA* firmly clutched in my hand. Because the tide was running out, I had to stand up on the stern rail of our boat to get to the top of the wall. It was wet and slippery on the dock and I could find nothing to tie to. The outgoing tide was pulling *RABASKA* toward a German vessel off our bow. I looked to see how the other boats were secured and realized the ring was about three feet down the side of the stonewall.

Still dressed in my cumbersome *house* I leaned over to run the stern line through the ring, when I realized my sea legs were not suitable for solid land. I could not let go of the rope because of our proximity to the other vessels but the dock seemed to be going up and down under me. I was about to go head first into the harbor. I shouted for Peter, who quickly came up behind me, put his arms around my body, and held onto me as I secured the line in the ring. We were tied to shore at last. The time was 0300.

No sooner were we secure than the skipper of the boat in front of us appeared on deck and invited us for coffee. We were a pretty scruffy looking bunch and not dressed to go visiting our new neighbors in the early hours of the morning. He insisted we come at once.

Below on his yacht I was astonished at the luxury. The skipper, another German whose name was Peter, was a little drunk. He and his mate, now asleep in the aft cabin, had arrived a few hours before us and had spent their first night ashore in the Café Sport. He advised Henk to call the Customs and Immigration immediately. He said they were very strict, and even if we only left a message, we would be accounted for till morning.

While Henk went back to the boat to call, the skipper of the German yacht produced fresh apples and oranges. He was obviously a man with ocean experience. He knew exactly what our bodies craved. Fresh fruit was a magnificent treat and, after a final schnapps, we headed back to *RABASKA* for a few hours of sleep before daylight. We had been at sea for eighteen days or two and a half weeks.

Chapter 20

THE AZORES HAVE A subtropical climate. The winters are mild and the summers very comfortable. One nice thing is that the air is clean and driven by the warm waters of the Gulf Stream. What we had discovered coming into the harbor in the early morning was that it is not unusual for clouds to form around the tops of the mountains and then come down the slope to blanket the water.

I was the first one up in the morning and immediately put on the coffee pot. What a pleasure to be able to use the stove and not worry about things flying around the cabin. While the pot was boiling, I pushed back the hatch cover and looked up onto the pier. Staring down at me was a uniformed man wearing a gun. I waved to him, gave him a smile, and went back to my coffee making. As the German Peter said the night before, "There will be a hundred eyes watching your every move." I rousted the skipper from the quarter berth and told him about the man in uniform. The skipper decided to go immediately to the government office on the other side of the harbor to present our papers.

Directly above us on the dock where I had earlier seen the man in uniform, were three men loading a container of fruit onto a truck. I turned on my ancient mariner smile once more and waved a greeting. I was rewarded immediately with some fresh pears that had *accidentally* broken out of the wooden boxes.

When Henk returned to the boat, he informed us that not only had he cleared with the government office, but he had also made arrangements at the marina on the other side of the harbor.

We managed to get the motor going again and moved over to the marina location. There were hundreds of sailboats from all over the world packed into the marina basin. *RABASKA* was one of the smallest and least equipped.

We ended up rafted fourth from the stonewall. We were not able to use shore power as we were not equipped for European standards, but there was plenty of fresh water available.

We immediately began to clean up the boat. We took everything out of the lockers and washed them down with fresh water from the dock. While things were drying in the warm morning sun, we headed down the dock. Although getting a hot shower should have been our first priority, we set out along the main street looking and, no doubt smelling, like three unshaven, grimy skid-row characters. Our destination was the Café Sport run by Jose Azevedo. We heard on the dock that this was the local watering hole and contact point for skippers and crew. Keeping in mind the time change, we wanted to call home and report our safe arrival in Horta.

THE PHONE IN CAFÉ Sport was on a little counter next to the bar. Apparently, there was always a line-up of sailors waiting to report their safe arrival, or arranging for new crew. Finally, it was my turn. Maureen answered the phone after the first ring.

What a thrill to hear her voice. Unfortunately, I had to keep the conversation short, and because I was surrounded by tough ocean sailors waiting their turn, I am ashamed to say that I was unable to say what was in my heart, but only that I would call again.

After we all had a turn on the phone we left the bar and headed for the first restaurant. The locals on the narrow street along the waterfront did not seem to take notice of our appearance. Visiting sailors probably accounted for a good portion of their summer tourism business.

We found a small restaurant and after a long consultation with the waiter, we ordered a huge fish platter and three bottles of local beer. We left the restaurant and returned immediately to the marina. I grabbed my toilet kit, a towel and a pack of clean clothes and headed for the shower room—oh the joys of civilization! I felt that it was a new beginning, a sort of rebirth, as I headed back to the boat—beard trimmed, hair washed, and wearing dry, clean clothes.

Although it was good to be on land again and to be able to walk around, we had to spend a lot of time on the boat attempting to get it sea ready for the next leg. First, everything came out on deck in an attempt to dry out the cabin. Even after two days, things left out to dry, were still damp when returned to the cabin after sunset. My sleeping bag, hung carefully over the boom each day, went from very wet the first night, to very damp the second night, and finally to slightly damp on the third night. I think that could be defined as progress.

While the boom and cabin roof were covered with drying items, we were busy removing the jib-sheet tracks from the deck. They ran along each side of the boat for about ten feet and were used to hold the lines that control the jib sail. Because they were bolted through the deck, it was necessary to remove the inside paneling on the coach-house roof as well, and empty all upper cupboards of their contents. There were bolts every five inches along each track. Each was removed and fresh silicone caulking applied, and the bolt and nut tightened back into place. At the same time, Peter put a line of caulking along the undersides of the teak trim on each side of the boat's rail. A good deal of attention was also given to the chain-plates. One porthole cover, which was found to be loose, was tightened and re-caulked. This explained the rust on our Force 10 heater.

Naturally we removed the mast collar, cut new hardwood pegs, and drove them top down between the mast and the deck, where we hoped they could no longer fall out. We expected this would stop the terrible mast motion as well as the endless screeching sounds that had accompanied us that far into the voyage. We replaced the waterproof collar to keep the inside of the boat dry. This work took the best of three days. Our hope was that the boat would be watertight at the end of all these repairs.

As a reward for our work, the skipper treated us to dinner at a hotel that was a converted castle overlooking the harbor. It was a great treat, especially for the cook! After dinner, Henk called his daughter in Toronto who arranged for a replacement part for the engine. We had been told earlier by the local Mid-Atlantic Marina that it would take two to three weeks to secure the part. We had no intention of remaining that long in Horta. The skipper's call to Toronto confirmed they could have the part sent in a matter of days, to Ponta Delgada on San Miguel Island, our next port of call,

WHILE WORKING ON THE boat it was interesting to watch yachts coming in off the ocean. A large German vessel motored past us one day with two adults and three small children on-board. You could see the relief and joy in their faces as they tied their boat securely to the wall.

Another yacht, a converted Maxi racing boat, pulled in next to us one afternoon. No sooner were they secured, than one crewmember jumped onto the dock, sea bag in hand, and gave the skipper the middle finger salute. As he marched down the dock, the "F" word could clearly be heard in his mutterings about the competency of the skipper. I don't think they had a pleasant trip from New York!

Later we were tied alongside the same Maxi and had to walk across their deck to get to their dock. The deck was over twenty-feet wide. There were winches as big as oil drums and jib sheet tracks all over the deck. I was glad we did not have to check them out for leaks. The spinnaker poles, that have to be lifted into position in a race, were so large that it would take three or four crewmembers just to attach them to the mast.

We learned from the talk on the dock that the Maxi had left New York shortly after us. About eight hundred miles offshore they received a distress call from a Tartan 40 about two days ahead of them. The Tartan had lost its rudder. The posts holding the rudder had broken, and the rudder became unhinged and sank.

I spent some time later talking to the skipper of the Tartan 40 and he told me they had experienced trouble with the rudder earlier in the trip. They made a makeshift replacement as backup. When they lost their rudder, they attached the provisional one, but during the major storm, it also broke away. Not only were they unable to steer the boat, but the vessel seriously began to take on water. Fortunately, they were able to maintain radio contact with the Maxi until it caught up to them.

In the meantime, the crew checked out the boat. The rudderpost had not pulled through the stern and they were not able to locate another source of the leak. They had to man the pumps twenty-four hours a day to keep the Tartan 40 afloat until help arrived.

When the Maxi caught up to them, the crew abandoned their vessel. It was too rough to bring one boat up beside the other, so using their rubber dingy they transported the crew from the sinking vessel to the Maxi. One and a half hours later the Tartan 40 sank. The skipper told me he could only watch until the water reached the coach-house roof, and then he had to go below on the Maxi.

What was sad about this sinking was that the owner was originally a native of Horta and was returning to his birthplace from the United

States. As a small boy, he dreamed that one day he would be the proud owner of a beautiful yacht and return to his home harbor. That day arrived, but he was robbed of his chance to bring it into the harbor for his family and friends to enjoy.

On another day a Freedom 39, a boat without stays and shrouds to support the mast, docked directly behind us. There were two masts, one of the them being very close to the bow of the boat. The sail was partially wrapped around this mast, and because a fierce squall was whipping through the harbor, the sail was flapping violently. The skipper made no effort to stop the noise that was a nuisance for all of us. Apparently during a storm the un-stayed mast had made a half turn, binding the halyard. Because there were no steps on the mast, or any shrouds to climb on, it was impossible for them to get the sail down.

Two young men on the dock volunteered to climb the mast and attempt to lower the sail. They were beaten back each time by the flaying canvas. They soon abandoned their efforts, and by morning, there were just shreds of material flapping in the light breeze. I met the local sail maker the next morning and I said, "Good morning, Mr. Sail Maker." His reply was, "In a place like this, I am not a sail maker, only a sail repair man."

THE WEATHER WAS NOT the temperate, maritime climate characterized by agreeable temperatures as peddled in the tourist brochures. Judging from the agricultural nature of the island and the presence of small palm trees, I am sure that statement was normally true. During our brief stay in Horta, the weather was cold, with a light fine mist every few hours coming down from the top of the surrounding hill making it difficult to dry out our boat. In fact, it was necessary to get whatever was drying on the deck, below, two or three times a day. When we left the boat to go into town, everything had to be put below till our return. That strange little mountain at the end of the harbor was often enshrouded in its white fog as it was on the night of our arrival. Those who lived high up above the harbor were often rendered invisible in the heavy mists. Every now and again, a fierce wind came in off the ocean. It was necessary to make sure the boat was well secured. We finally had to run a line from our boat to the rocky point at the end of the pier. The locals told us it was winter weather, although it was supposed to be summer in the Azores.

The hills that surround the town are divided by low hedges. From a distance, it appeared as if nothing but grass was growing in these squares. It looked like Prince Edward Island from the air. There were few signs of poverty. The prosperity of the island rests in agriculture, the breeding of livestock and fishing. A most beautiful sight was the 6,000-foot volcano directly across from us on Pico Island. It was not always visible because of the constant fog, but when it was, it was surrounded by a white halo. It is called Pico Alto to distinguish it from the many smaller volcanoes that are scattered around the island. It was a constant reminder that those islands were originally formed by volcanic eruptions.

For a few days we were tied up to a boat from Florida. One morning I went shopping with the skipper's wife. She showed me the best places to buy supplies, pointed out the sidewalk vegetable and fruit stands, the nearest bakery and the supermarket. I began to replace our food supply and to purchase more vegetables, fruit, eggs and meat. The island also had wonderful sourdough bread and fresh cheese.

One evening we returned to the Café Sport to meet other sailors, and exchange stories and experiences. The information learned in these discussions was invaluable. Knowing how others dealt with the temperament of the sea, and what they did to survive, was exciting and instructive.

We met another skipper from Toronto who had been out cruising for the past three years. He had a hired crew that he had picked up along the way. His present crew consisted of a young British girl, and a tall, lanky Dutchman named Tony. It turned out Tony had been in the army in Holland, as had Henk in his youth, so they hit it off from the beginning. In retrospect, I think Tony was looking for a new berth, as the atmosphere between Tony and the British girl was very tense.

THE MOST OUTSTANDING CHARACTERISTIC about the breakwater that protected the marina from the ocean was its famous paintings. The wall and the dock itself were completely covered with paintings left behind by visiting boats. Some of them are pieces of art. Henk wanted us to buy some paint and leave our own art somewhere on the wall.

The breakwater was easily the length of three football fields, about fifty feet wide, and had a built up section on the ocean side. Every square inch of this dock and wall was covered with colorful pictures.

To leave our mark we had to paint over one that had been obliterated by weather and time. We went searching for just such a spot. One rather large painting or memorial read:

> *"If you want to have fun for one day—*
> *get drunk*
> *If you want to have fun for a week—get*
> *married*
> *If you want to have fun for life—get a*
> *sailboat."*

At a nearby paint store, obviously familiar with would-be artists anxious to leave their mark, we purchased a few small cans of paint. We returned to the spot we found on the wall and using masking tape, we outlined a spot about two feet square. We sprayed it white. When the paint dried, using an old toothbrush, Peter painted a copy of our club burgee in gold and blue with the words *RABASKA, TORONTO 1996*. We were not as vain as some yachtsmen who not only drew maps of where they had been, but included the name of each member of the crew.

Even though most of the five days we were docked in Horta were spent repairing the boat, we found time to walk around the town, see the sights and discover some fine restaurants. Best of all, were the long still nights with no black watch and relatively dry and motionless berths to sleep in.

Our last act in Horta was to do laundry and top-up our fresh water supply. We were ready for the second leg, from Horta to San Miguel, the most easterly island of the Archipelago.

Chapter 21

On sunday morning we left the marina in Horta. We were almost a month from home and anxious to continue our journey. Instead of going out between Faial and Pico, the route we had come in, we decided to sail across the six-mile gap between the two islands and then down between the islands of Pico and San Jorge, a channel eight miles wide. On the chart, this looked as if it would be the shortest route and the best choice. The waves were running three to five feet between the islands but the wind, coming in from the northwest, was strong and gusty.

Since we were closer to the shoreline of Pico, the top of its principal volcano was very conspicuous. The smaller volcanoes could be seen on the top of the low peaks. For miles along the coast, village after village had little white homes with red tile roofs. Every town had its own church. Pico Island itself is forty-eight kilometers long and fifteen kilometers wide. The sides of the hills are terraced and cultivated, reminding me of the farms in Italy. The crops on Pico were apples, pears, apricots, peaches, plums and oranges. It was also once a great wine producing place, but their vines were attacked by disease in the late 19th century. They say Vinho do Pico was famous but I could not find any in the local stores in Horta. At one time, Pico was also a whaling center but that industry was closed in the 1970s. The coast itself is very rugged, with few harbors, and no beaches. The shores of San Jorge, on our port side, appeared much the same.

Although the distance from one end of this beautiful stretch of water to the other is approximately 600 kilometers, the distance between Faial and San Miguel was only one hundred and forty-four nautical miles. We hoped to arrive at the city of Ponta Delgada sometime after lunch on the second day.

At noon the wind died completely and I took the opportunity to prepare some Sunday lunch. We had no sooner finished than the wind returned with a vengeance from the southeast. It came sweeping down the slopes of Pico, turning the water black as it raced toward us. We immediately had to shorten sail. The wind was over 40 knots as we struggled to keep the boat upright. Then, just as suddenly, the wind would die and settle in again at 8 knots. We had to put out more sail to keep the boat moving against the tide. But as soon as we settled down another black spot would appear coming out from the shore, and the next squall would strike the boat. This strange condition kept up for the full length of the islands and it was not till 1815 that we finally cleared land and entered the open sea once again. Away from the land, the wind was once more very light, but since night was falling, we decided to lower the mainsail and continue under jib alone.

When I went below to get some sleep before my first watch I was disappointed to find everything that we had so carefully dried in Horta, was wet and damp again. There were no visible leaks, but the salt in the cushions and sleeping bags attracted the moisture in the air. The black watch was cold and damp and once again, I was dressed in my survival suit that was still referred to as Dick's *house*. Very few fishing boats were visible during the watch, nor were there any dolphins to entertain me.

In the morning we were all on deck by 0600, drinking coffee and looking forward to the sight of land. We had traveled over a hundred nautical miles and there were only forty miles to our destination.

I knew the skipper was concerned about the motor problem and was hoping against hope that the spare part would be waiting for us. The tension showed at times. However, unlike some skippers we encountered, who treated crew as passengers, we had learned to work collaboratively as a team.

As a crewmember, I can appreciate the contribution a crew makes to any passage. While it is true one can sail across the ocean alone, it is also true that it can only be done under extreme hardship. It should also be pointed out that the skipper and owner of a yacht has the most to lose and thus, has greater responsibility. However, with a crew, even though there are irksome moments, both physically and psychologically, the stress factors are greatly reduced. Not only is there human companionship but everyone gets more sleep, someone is there to do the cooking, to trim sail, to navigate, and as a team, survive the worst mother nature can throw at them.

On those rare occasions when the atmosphere was tense, Peter dealt with the situation with humor. I simply ignored it. I usually managed to put on a happy face, and say to myself, "It does not matter." A bruised ego is easily rehabilitated. If there was some truth to criticism, then I had something to learn. If not, my own self-confidence based on experience, was strong enough to heal the wound quickly. In a small boat, an open confrontation is dangerous and creates a plague that is difficult to eradicate. This passive attitude enabled me to understand the extent of my dependence on the other crewmembers. Most of all, it empowered me to quickly return to the positive side of our experiences, and to enjoy the uniqueness of my crewmates.

I FINALLY LEARNED HOW to manage in the galley. I found some small rubber mats about one foot square hidden away in a small locker. They were made of the material used to keep rugs from slipping on hardwood floors. When spread out on the counter top they did not slide, and pots, open cans, plates, cups, and an assortment of other things, remained firm some of the time.

From the very beginning, I could see that neither Henk nor Peter was interested in giving a lot of thought to the provisioning of the boat. Indeed, in our conversations, as I tried to discern their likes and dislikes, I learned that they were willing and able to eat whatever came out of a can. Canned meat, beans and soup, which may do for a short journey, did not cause my mouth to salivate. They thought these goods, along with whatever fresh produce we could pick up in New York, would be more than adequate. Peter made it clear that he did not like anything cooked with fresh garlic or olive oil, my two favorite aids to mouth watering foods. Their nonchalant attitude towards food allowed me to plan a menu that would suit my palate. I did not have to worry about Dutch or German specialties. But there was no way I was going to eat bully beef or sausages out of a can for weeks on end.

The only criterion Henk insisted on was that we not fall short of food. If for some reason we found ourselves adrift without sail or power, he wanted to be sure the boat was well stocked. I was instructed as cook in waiting, to provision the boat for seventy days. If all went well we would be able to cross the ocean and do some cruising in the Mediterranean. He wanted to allow for a wide margin of error.

LIMITING MYSELF TO PREPARING one dish at a time while at sea also reduced the number of items left on the counter top. And perhaps the most important skill I learned was how to brace myself and keep both hands free. For example, on a port tack I rested one side of my butt on the counter top, stretching my right leg across to the divider between the navigation station and the port berth. In that position, I was secure enough to peel potatoes or open a can. In fact, I got so accustomed to preparing food in that position, it took two days for me to break the habit when in port.

Years ago when I was involved in long distance racing, I used to run a safety harness through the handrail above the galley stove and suspend myself off the sole of the boat. This way I could swing back and forth like the stove in front of me, and have both hands to do the cooking. I would not recommend this method on the ocean. The motion of the boat is far more irregular and unpredictable. Besides, *RABASKA* had no handrails in the galley area.

Chapter 22

WHEN WE FINALLY SIGHTED the east end of San Miguel, the wind began to diminish. With only ten miles to go, we lost the wind completely. Finally, the skipper decided to try the motor. It only worked for five minutes when it overheated and had to be shut off. Peter's repairs had moved us in and out of Horta without incident, but failed to take us any distance without quitting. An attempt to attach a water pump borrowed from the fresh water system worked briefly. Unfortunately, the pump fell from its mount and the small plastic cogs that moved the belt, shattered. Once again, we were without power and close to shore. Henk tried calling the Marina in Ponta Delgada to see if we could get a tow but there was no answer. It was a religious holiday we found out later, and everything was closed. He thought about calling one of the many small boats moving in and out of the harbor in the distance. We convinced him to try the DRS and see if we could get closer to shore.

By late afternoon, we were slowly moving along the south side of the island. Although we were five miles off the coast, we could see the breakers along the rocky shore. We were caught in two rip tides that made our progress even slower. When we were finally within two miles of the harbor, we spotted a white sailboat motoring toward the entrance. We thought it looked like one we had seen in Horta, so Henk called on the radio, "Sailboat, sailboat entering Ponta Delgada harbor." A heavily accented voice replied and when we told the captain our problem, he said he would stand by the harbor entrance and wait for us.

As we watched the white sailboat it motored right past the breakwater and disappeared into the harbor behind a large hill. About ten minutes later, we heard the accented voice on the radio calling us. He informed us that he was a rather large vessel and that he would have difficulty maneuvering us into the harbor, but that he was willing to try. Then we saw for the first time the boat that had returned our call. It was not the white sailboat at all. It was a large, green, wooden Swiss fishing boat.

When we were close to the fishing boat we dropped the DRS. The captain came up and threw us a line. We attached it to the bow cleat and he began pulling us. We had to be very careful because, for some reason, we kept catching up to him. Finally, he let go the bowline and we came up alongside, as his crew was busy dropping large fenders along the side of their boat. Then he moved in and secured a bow and stern line, and we were literally dragged into the harbor.

On our towboat, there were about twelve young men. The skipper was an older man and there was one woman on deck as well. The crew seemed to take orders from another young man, who must have been the first mate. We soon learned they spoke German and Peter broke the ice and started up a conversation in a much more relaxed atmosphere.

They towed us toward the customs dock and then let us go, giving us enough of a push to get us to the dock. We used the motor for a minute, just in case we needed to make a quick maneuver and tied up behind the white sailboat we had tried to contact earlier. It was a Hunter 44 on its way from Florida to Israel.

While Henk was clearing us at customs, I was standing on the dock near *RABASKA*. A man came up from behind me and said, "From Bluffers Park Yacht Club, eh?" I immediately turned to meet the skipper of *O'SEAN* out of Port Credit Yacht Club in Ontario. What a small world!

I also met a young woman who was patiently waiting for the green boat that had towed us into port. She was disappointed that it did not dock, as the young first mate was her boyfriend. The boat had moved back into the harbor looking for a place to drop anchor.

She told me the name of the boat was *TECONA* and that the crew was composed of drug addicts on a nine-month rehabilitation cruise, and that the woman was the therapist. The customs finally radioed *TECONA* and told them to come into the dock and tie up behind us. When they were secure, Henk thought it would be a good idea to take the crew out for some beer. I suggested he limit his largess to the captain.

When Henk checked with the marina office for the replacement part for our Volvo motor he was told that it did not arrive. He spotted a package on the desk behind the counter, and when he asked about it, he was told that it was for an American. Henk insisted on seeing it anyway. When the attendant showed it to him, his name and the name of the boat were clearly marked on the package. His daughter had come through. We had our much-needed part. Henk and Peter immediately installed it and arranged for repairs to the broken fresh water pump as well. We were back in business, and we moved the boat off the customs dock to a much more comfortable finger dock.

While all of this was going on, I baked chocolate cookies and bread in preparation for the next leg of our journey. The crew ate all of the cookies in one sitting—so much for planning ahead.

THE CITY OF PONTA Delgada is quite beautiful. It is the most populous city in the Azores and possesses tall buildings mixed with more traditional dwellings of architectural value. The two styles blend together to create a very pleasant walk along the waterfront. Almost everything is made from volcanic stone, including the paving blocks on the roads and streets. The black and white volcanic bricks are interwoven to create a beautiful pattern. While getting my daily exercise I passed a group of workers, sitting on well-worn blocks of wood, and wearing a huge leather glove on one hand, chipping and laying stones on the sidewalk. When you consider the miles of roads and sidewalks, and the millions of little stones neatly inlaid they represent a lot of jobs.

The weather forecasts that were coming in were not good. There was a strong indication that a high had settled between San Miguel and Gibraltar, said to be causing a calm spot 700 miles long. No one could predict how long it would last, so the skipper purchased two extra drums of engine fuel and strapped them to the foot of the mast, something we said we would never do. If this high were to continue, we discussed sailing above the calm and then back down the Gulf Stream to Gibraltar.

The white sailboat that preceded us into the harbor was moored close to us and we soon became friends with the owner and one of his crew. Jacob, the young crewman, had just completed five years as a diver with the Israeli army. He took a liking to us and spent a lot of time talking about his experiences. He was in a difficult position as his skipper also had a wife and daughter on-board. Jacob was the odd-one out and constantly found himself in an uncomfortable situation.

Like the harbor in Horta, the harbor at Ponta Delgada was filled with visiting sailors. The condition of some of the vessels, along with the stories that go with them, were tales of hardship and even disaster. The day after we left the customs dock, a small sailboat arrived under power. It was flying the British flag. The skipper had died three days earlier from bleeding ulcers and the crew had brought the boat safely into the harbor.

The authorities appeared from everywhere, police, doctors, ambulance attendants, along with radio and TV reporters. The situation was complicated. It was a British vessel entering a foreign port. The Azores was granted the status of an Autonomous Region, and self-government was instituted in 1976. The regional government is located in Ponta Delgada, thus so much bureaucracy. Discussions around the docks had to do with the proof of death. Perhaps the crew thought their skipper was some kind of Captain Bligh. At any rate, the negotiations lasted three hours before the body was finally removed from the boat and taken away in the ambulance.

There were a number of disabled vessels either tied up along the far side of the breakwater or sitting in cradles on top of the dock. One beautiful yacht was sitting there minus its mast. The owners had lost everything overboard and had to rig a sail, using the boom as a mast, to claw their way into port. It was a sad sight, but encouraging to know that the possibility exists.

MOORED NEXT TO US was a yawl that looked as if it had been stepped on by a giant. The boat had done a complete rollover during a storm. The dodger, the two masts and sails had been ripped from the boat and lost. The pulpit, the stainless steel rail on the front of the boat, was flattened onto the deck. At one time, I would not have believed that it was possible just from the force of the waves alone, but there was the proof before my eyes.

The boat now had a new main mast donated by another vessel in port and a wooden stick for the second mast. Both were held up with wire and whatever else the owner could find around the marina.

The skipper's name was Manfred. One day we were sitting below in *RABASKA* having a shot to warm our spirits when Manfred told us his story in broken English and German.

Originally Manfred was from Rostock, East Germany, famous for its university, its shipbuilding and mechanical engineering. He left there about three years earlier on a trip to Brazil. I don't know what his trade was, but he was some sort of engineer who worked with boats back in Europe. His nephew was looking after the business.

He took his boat down the coast of Africa, crossed the ocean below the equator, and then down to Brazil as far as the Amazon. Because the Amazon is so big, he got stuck in the currents. The mouth of the river is over a hundred miles wide, and the current was coming down at over eight knots. When he made progress up to the river, he would only get pushed back into the ocean. This went on for a number of days. By that time, his food supplies were low and his fresh water was totally gone. Manfred took all the pots and pans on the boat, filled them with seawater and covered them with plastic wrap. At the end of each day, he collected the dew on the plastic covers. He was able to accumulate about a cup of fresh water each day.

Finally, he found the backwater, the current that would take him up the river. He was using the charts he brought from Europe, but they were dated. The sand banks on the charts did not match the ever changing ones in the river. Manfred soon found himself stuck on a sand bank in the river mouth. Since it was near evening, he threw out his anchor and slept till the next day.

When he woke up in the morning he saw two men trying to steal his life raft. He grabbed his machete that he carried in the cockpit and chased them. But while he was securing the raft to the boat, another group of men showed up with guns. Manfred grabbed a portable phone and held it to his ear and pretended he was calling the police. The phone did not work because he had previously lost its antenna, but the would-be-thieves did not know that and they took off.

Later in the day, five men arrived in a small fishing boat and offered to tow him off the sand bank. After some negotiation, they got a line aboard Manfred's vessel and pulled him clear of the sand. When in midstream Manfred invited them aboard to show his appreciation. They came aboard and pulled out a sub-machine gun, a shotgun and a pistol. They immediately stole everything they could get their hands on, his radio, batteries, lifeboat and motor, passport and about twenty-thousand dollars in American funds. He was afraid for his life as the 17-year-old youth with the men appeared very nervous as he held the shotgun to Manfred's face. When they were leaving his boat, he asked them why fishermen would do such a thing. They replied it was because he had so much and they had so little. He then asked them how he was to survive and the leader threw him a fresh fish. But the fish flew over the side of the boat and disappeared in the water. The fisherman/thief then gave him another fish.

When he finally arrived at a small town, he reported to the local authorities, giving them a description of the men and their boat. That seemed to be the end of it.

A few days later Manfred met a local newsman who spoke German. Manfred told him his story and it was published the next day in the local paper. The article questioned why the police were not doing anything to help. Apparently, the people in that area wanted to maintain good relations with Germany, and they were upset with what had happened to Manfred. The story was picked up by other papers and soon made coverage on local TV stations. Many people came and gave him food and supplies.

As a result of all this publicity, a few weeks later Manfred was summoned to the police station. When he arrived, he was taken to the basement and there, on the floor, was everything that had been stolen from his boat. He asked the police if they had recovered any money. They replied that his money was gone. When he asked about the robbers, he learned that the police had shot them. Manfred was upset and told them the few stolen possessions were not worth the death of some poor fishermen. He later learned that the police, who are very poorly paid themselves, had taken the money and killed the thieves to keep them quiet. The fact that one of them was only seventeen bothered Manfred for months after.

He finally got his boat provisioned and started the trip back to Germany. Somewhere around the 42nd parallel in mid-ocean, he went below to get a cup of coffee. He was sitting on a bunk drinking the coffee, when suddenly the whole boat turned upside down. When it righted itself, he was up to his knees in water. He said he was never so busy in his life as he grabbed a bucket and began bailing. For him, the sad story was that in Brazil someone had given him a little dog. It was sitting under the dodger when the boat was hit by the squall and the dog was lost. You could see the tears in Manfred's eyes when he talked about how he was attached to that pup.

On deck everything was gone, his masts, his sails and his dodger. He drifted around for a couple of days when a German freighter with a Russian crew and captain hove into sight. They came alongside and took Manfred off his boat, treated him to hot food and a shower. But Manfred was not willing to abandon his vessel. So some of the ship's crew made him a little wooden mast and provided him with some provisions. Off he went again only to be picked up by another freighter, which took him in tow. After a short time, the towline broke, and Manfred again refused to abandon his boat. It took him another twenty days to get into Ponta Delgada where we met him.

As we heard this story I could not help but think, how fortunate we had been and what we had endured. But at the same time, parts of his story seemed to stretch the truth. Nevertheless, his vessel was there and his situation was very real.

One of the other visiting boats donated a mizzenmast, and the crew of another yacht located a mast somewhere and set it up on Manfred's boat. He seemed deeply appreciative. Now that he had the wooden mast from the freighter and the main mast, all that he needed was sails. Henk gave him an extra storm jib we had on *RABASKA*. Manfred's eyes lit up like search lights when he saw that the sail was new and never used.

Manfred left soon after and we hoped he made it back to Germany safely, for he was determined to do just that.

WE SPENT SOME TIME visiting the port and exploring the inner workings of a huge fishing boat. One night after a dinner of steaks marinated in beer, I decided to turn in early. Peter and Henk grabbed a bottle of schnapps and headed out to visit the skipper of *TECONA,* the vessel that had towed us into port. They had no sooner left when Jacob came on-board wanting to go to a local carnival that had been set up near the marina. I declined the invitation. I had just turned out the cabin light when Henk and Peter returned and dragged me out of my berth to, "Come and see the cultural show at the carnival."

The four of us ended up in the beer tent listening to the local music provided by a group of teenagers. They sang and played traditional music and their performance was excellent. I was very tired so I excused myself and returned to the boat. I did not hear the rest of the crew come aboard later.

The next day we continued to replenish our stores, especially careful to buy plenty of fruit juice and pop. Henk again treated us to a great dinner where we met a group of touring Americans. Our spirits were good, but we were anxious to set sail and finish our journey. Talk around the docks was that our last leg would be a cakewalk. I thought that perhaps shorts and sunscreen would be in order for the remainder of the trip. Was I wrong!

Chapter 23

WE TOPPED UP THE water, cleared customs and left the harbor at Ponta Delgada at noon. We motored for an hour to recharge the batteries, and then, once again, we were under sail. As we neared the far end of the island in the late afternoon, we were hit by a strong wind out of the east, the direction we wanted to sail. For that reason, we had to keep flying the main in order to remain close to our course. We noticed another sailboat come out of Ponta Delgada and begin to tack behind us.

As the wind increased, we were forced to put a reef in the mainsail. Unfortunately, in the process some of the reef points were tied in the wrong place, and when we pulled the old sail back up it ripped in two places.

After supper, we stripped the main from the boom and dragged it, soaking wet, below. It was too rough to sit on the coach-house roof to mend, so we had to get the sail below deck. Again, Peter did the sewing and I held a flashlight. It took over two hours to mend the sail and when we finished, we stuffed it in the quarter berth for the night.

Our greatest disappointment was that after all of our hard work repairing the boat in Horta, once on the open sea, the boat began to leak as before. To make matters worse, the mast had already begun to screech and howl. With nine hundred nautical miles to go, we had the same annoying conditions our first day out of the Azores.

As I sat my first black watch that night, it seemed as if our sojourn ashore had never happened. We were back to the challenge of fighting the sea. I spotted one freighter that night, but the sailboat that followed us out from Ponta Delgada was no longer in sight ahead of us. Unfortunately, as I prepared to go on deck for the second watch I discovered I was suffering from a serious case of the trots. Perhaps too much fresh fruit while ashore.

There was not much changed in the head and a balancing act was still required. With the boat on a port tack, it was a Herculean task to remain balanced on the head. It was even more difficult to draw the flush water in from the ocean because of the heel of the boat. I repeated my earlier mistake and pumped too vigorously, causing the contents of the bowl to spray both the floor and me. This time Henk had to come to my rescue with a bucket of water from the stern. After cleaning up, I found the Imodium and prayed that it would do its job.

Later, on deck, Henk and I got the mainsail out of the quarter berth and attached it to the mast and boom. We decided on a permanent reef and spent some time getting it right. We wanted to eliminate stress points that would damage the sail again. We also felt it was necessary to get good trim so that the sail would hold its best shape and carry us forward into the wind. Next, we cautiously removed the mast collar and drove even more pegs into position hoping to stabilize the mast in place.

The wind was forcing us below the rhumb line, and we knew we would be sailing further south pushed by the strong current as well. We discussed whether we should tack immediately to gain ground, or hope for a change in the wind direction. Being forced too far south would mean some heavy tacking later to get back up to Gibraltar, adding days and miles to our trip.

So much for sunscreen and shorts! Again, we found ourselves in high waves, strong winds, wet spray and a very sodden cabin. Our disposition had been put to the test in our first leg of the journey to the Azores. We were not prepared for a repeat of those awful conditions. After all, we had been promised a dry boat, warm sun and fair weather. What we were getting was another thrashing from the sea.

I said that one reason for taking the trip was to experience the hardships of the early immigrants on their journey to America. It was now truly happening to me. I was sick with the runs, wet, cold and already tired of the constant pounding of the boat. For the first time I felt I wanted the trip to end. I was trapped and unable to free myself from the boat; hardships that somehow were manageable on the first leg now only seemed insurmountable.

I turned in early hoping to get a few hours sleep before being called on deck for the bloody middle watch. The crew was good to me once more and when I awoke, the day was already breaking. Knowing how exhausting that diarrhea can be, they had pity on me, and let me sleep through the night. I felt a little better as I climbed into my survival suit and went on deck to relieve Peter.

The sea reminded me of the tabletop on a pinball machine. As far as we could see in every direction, there were rainstorms, like huge mushrooms looming up out of the sea. Our little boat, like the steel pinball, bounced between the storms, every now and again getting caught by one of them.

That was the longest tack I had ever experienced. For twenty-four hours, we did not make one adjustment to the sails and with the self-steering device guiding the boat—we all became merely passengers.

Like the first few days out of New York, we fell back into the old pattern of eat, sleep and duty watch. It was too rough to do anything else. We were exhausted even though we seemed to be getting lots of sleep off watch. I don't think the effects of the sleep were the same because of the constant body movement in the berth. If the motion of the boat had been less violent, perhaps the effects on our sleep would not have been so profound. However, as before, even in sleep we had to hold on.

We only saw one ship in the distance that night and the sea, devoid of any life, was cold and lonely. There were no man-of-war jellyfish, no dolphins to frolic at our bow, no whales or turtles, and only one or two birds. All these creatures of the sea somehow made the journey less lonesome before. Now we realized how much we missed them all.

We continued to remain on the port tack. The winds were hovering at twenty knots, but gusting in the passing storms to thirty and thirty-five. Rainshowers were followed by clearings and magnificent cloud formations and configurations. With a little imagination I could see all kinds of creatures glaring down at us. Could the fears of the early seamen really have a foundation in reality after all? Or was it just my exhausted body that played havoc with my mind?

That evening at sunset there were two round holes, or small openings, in the gargantuan black clouds behind us. The rays of the setting sun shimmering through the misty air resembled the piercing eyes of some heavenly monster glaring down at me. It was surreal and in my imagination I saw a furious and fuming tiger. The clouds shifted their position and seemed to suddenly sprout leg-like columns. As the sun continued to drop below the horizon, the monsters lost their power and became nothing but black clouds blocking out the night stars and ushering in the darkness. I could not help but think this face of nature was an omen of things to come.

Chapter 24

THE NEXT MORNING WE sighted another ship. We called on the radio but they, like the previous ship, did not answer. It soon disappeared over the endless horizon never to be seen by us again. During our two stops in the Azores I made a point of talking to every skipper I met about the danger of ships on the ocean. I always got the same answer. "The ships may have radar, and may even be keeping watch on deck, although that is unlikely. So be vigilant, and above all don't fall asleep on watch and always be prepared to take evasive action."

Later in the day, I was changing into a pair of dry track pants that had been protected from the water in a green garbage bag. As I was attempting to struggle into them I again broke the cardinal rule of *hold on at all times*. I had braced the calves of my legs against the starboard berth, which pulls out like a drawer. I stood up and reached down with both hands to pull up my pants. Suddenly the boat took a severe lurch. The drawer-like bunk closed depriving me of my support, and my wet socks skidded on the sole of the cabin. Up in the air I flew and then down hard, striking my shinbones on the unyielding edge of the bunk. I could feel the pain shoot down both legs. I was stunned as I twisted and dropped backwards onto the narrow bunk hitting my back on some hard edge. I thought I might have done some serious damage, but I did not want to admit to the crew that I had fallen again. I thought they would think I was looking for favors and a reduced watch.

In a sense, I was lucky to hit my back where I did. A little higher and I might have broken a bone or crushed a kidney. When asked by Henk, who heard the crash on deck, if I was all right, I replied as if nothing had happened. It hurt a lot more than the previous bump on the head.

There was no sign of the windless hole that the weather forecasters in San Miguel predicted. Indeed, it was quite the opposite. The two jerry cans tied to the mast worked themselves loose a couple of times, and it was necessary to go on deck to tie them down. We were still on our port tack that day and the wind, the waves and the bad weather did not give up on us. The only advantage to their persistence was that they moved us closer to Gibraltar, called the Gib by most of the sailors we met. It appeared that we would have to fight all the way to keep the boat as close as possible to the rhumb line. We knew that if the winds persisted, we would reach the halfway mark some time the following day.

Before breakfast, the next day, the skipper decided to take a bath and clean the head. Given the state of the head and the galley, it was a wonder we had not contracted some awful disease. But with no fresh water for cleaning, and the constant dampness, it was very difficult to keep things trim and tidy.

To perform his ablutions, Henk fetched a pail of salt water from the stern of the boat, climbed down the companionway, slopping the water as he fought the motion of the boat. I was sitting on the starboard berth, the same one that had walloped me in the back. Relatively speaking it was now the only berth that was dry. I wanted to keep it that way. As Henk passed by me trying to balance himself and the bucket of water, I said, "Spill it on the deck, but don't spill any on this bunk. Please keep your bucket low." Suddenly the boat took one of its atypical lurches; the water flew out of the bucket and landed squarely in the middle of our one and only dry space. From then on there was nowhere to sit or lie down that was not very, very wet.

We began to pick up some voices on the VHF radio. Other mariners suggested that we keep the radio on when shipping or fishing vessels were about. Most of the talk we heard was Portuguese, but every now and again, we heard words in English. Because there was a lot of static, the transmissions tended to be broken up, meaning that we were still some distance from the boats. One thing I did hear however was, "There is a very serious situation in Pico—the winds have reached eighty-four kilometers." Thank God, Pico was over 400 nautical miles behind us. Since many of the vessels we met in Ponta Delgada had postponed their departure date till the so-called flat spot filled in with air, I wondered what they were saying as that wind lashed their peaceful resting harbor.

AT THIS TIME, I do not think that we were clinically depressed, but we certainly were low in spirit. This was by far the toughest part of our journey. There was nothing to change the daily routine; no distractions, no life in the sea, no sunshine, nothing to divert us from our misery. The crew was not eating and the conversation on deck each day centered on our frustration. The waves never seemed to tire of attacking us and I did not realize that crossing the North Atlantic in a small boat involved crossing a watery Alps as well. It seemed as if we had been climbing ever since we left New York.

Another challenge was to avoid dehydration. One would think that with all the water around us, and the dampness in the cabin, that this would be the least of our worries. But the careful use of our limited fresh water supply made us conscious of the need to drink plenty of liquids, such as juice, and to go easy on the schnapps. We fully realized that if we let our body fluids fall below a certain level that we could, theoretically, suffer from shock. The last thing we needed was to have the condition escalate to vomiting, diarrhea, and loss of fluid through our urine. I was particularly worried about this situation when I had my short bout of diarrhea.

I was reminded of Coleridge's famous lines from *The Rime of the Ancient Mariner:*

> *Water, water everywhere*
> *And all the boards did shrink*
> *Water, water, everywhere.*
> *Nor any drop to drink.*
> *The very deep did rot: O Christ*
> *That ever this should be!*
> *Yea, slimy things did crawl with legs*
> *Upon the slimy sea.*

Earlier in the year, I had picked up a bug when traveling in the Caribbean. I had a few days of diarrhea and was not able to keep anything in my body—liquid or food. On my return to Canada, I was taken to a hospital emergency room where they hooked me up on intravenous. So prior to leaving on the ocean crossing, I had purchased four large plastic bottles of Gatorade, and hidden them away in case anyone required a liquid that they could absorb quickly. After the first week out the crew would gather around the galley at dinner time to drink from an opened can, any liquid not needed for cooking. Our bodies constantly craved liquids and it was an item in limited supply.

Chapter 25

To be five days on the same tack was a unique experience, but I desperately needed a change, a change in wind direction, in wave action, in weather and in the signs of life about us. This part of the voyage became an endless chain of negative repetitive experiences.

Early that morning the wind strengthened and again we decided the mainsail had to come down. I got into my survival suit and after attaching my lifeline, crawled onto the coach-house roof. Peter stayed under the dodger to handle the lines and Henk crawled to the base of the mast to untie the halyard as I gathered the sail onto the boom.

While we were doing this, two giant waves swept over the boat and buried Henk and me in the salty brine. Although the force of the waves was sufficient to sweep us overboard, the one hand for the self rule kept us on the boat. The safety lines were an added consolation as we struggled to secure the sail from blowing over the side and into the water.

During the night, the wind continued to pick up and the waves were crashing more frequently over the bow and stern of the boat. Our tiny vessel would race down the side of one wave and then climb up the side of the next one. Now and again it would start up a wave, come to a sudden stop as a cresting surge would crash over the boat, causing the boat to pivot before it started down the other side. When this happened, the cockpit filled with water and I would get an unwanted bath. It was necessary for me to stay crouched behind the badly designed dodger for about ten minutes. Then, when I thought it was safe, I would stick my head up over the top of the dodger to take a quick look for ships. If the timing was right, I didn't get buckets of water thrown in my face.

The moon managed to appear in all of the turmoil and I had the opportunity to send love to Maureen, the only happy event in the evening. I had to wake Henk for the midnight watch even though I knew that he did not have the heart to face the forces of nature on deck one more time. But I had had my fill for one night and wanted to get below even if the bunk and sleeping bag awaiting me were wet.

THE NEXT MORNING WE passed the halfway mark. No one wanted breakfast. I made some coffee and had some dry black bread with jam. I also ate a bowl of bran cereal, with cold water to soften it up, in an attempt to get my system back in proper working order. The Imodium lived up to the promotional television spots, but now I needed help getting things back to normal.

From New York to the Azores, at least we had some weather that permitted us to open up the boat and air it out. We had no similar opportunity to air or clean the boat since we departed from Ponta Delgada. It was beginning to stink. Bodies, unwashed for five days, wet clothes hanging all over the cabin, a toilet that would not flush properly, and food going bad in the dirty galley, all contributed to the foul environment. We wanted to open the center hatch and let in some fresh air. But with the waves breaking over the bow, that was impossible. Even worse for me, the bran worked! I fetched a pail of water and poured it into the toilet bowl. As I prepared to sit down, the boat slammed into another huge wave, and the carefully placed water flew over me one more time. None of the other crew seemed to have these problems with the head!

Finally, for the first time since leaving San Miguel, we sighted some dolphins. To my dismay, they paid no attention to us, and they soon disappeared in the tall waves. Perhaps the stench was more than even they could stand. We hoped their presence was a sign that we had entered the Gulf Stream again, or the North Atlantic Drift, and with it a change in weather. I would have loved to get out of my survival suit if for no other reason, but to air it out.

At 1030 we spotted yet another freighter. This one was an American and we received an answer immediately. He gave us a weather report in a language we could understand. He said we would continue to get winds of Force #4 to Force #6, but that they would gradually veer to the north as we approached Gibraltar. He finished the weather report with, "I am always happy to assist a fellow mariner." Did that make us feel good! To be called a mariner by a professional sailor was indeed an honor. If the weather moved to the north, instead of fighting it all the time, we would be in a position to let the sail out and do a beam reach into Gibraltar. Our spirits immediately lifted.

I went below and asked Henk if I could turn on the heater to dry out the boat. He agreed, but when I tried to start it, it refused to light. The batteries were so low even the gas warning system refused to turn on. We had been unable to run the motor because of the rough seas, but we were now forced to charge up the batteries or we would not have running lights again during the night. We ran the motor long enough to get the system working again, but not long enough to damage it.

That night supper was a disaster. I tried using some kind of condensed milk to mix the dried potato pack. It was revolting. The Sea Cook was fine for boiling water and making soup. But when I tried to do something over low heat, it burnt whatever was in the pot. In other words, there was no low heat, so I had to hold the pot about three or four inches above the flame in order to get the pot to simmer. At the same time I had to have the usual firm grip on the boat.

By evening our spirits were once more flagging. Psychologically and physically we were simply rundown and out of gas. I tried to cheer myself up by doing another bath with handy-wipes. I even changed my shorts and T-shirt! It worked for a while, especially with the aid of one of Peter's schnapps. But the waves sounded as if they were trying to break up the boat, the racket below was terrible and it was next to impossible to do anything constructive. The fact that we were still getting along with one another was a magnificent tribute to the crew.

I YELLED AT PETER just before dinner time. The boat had been running for days with very few changes to the sails. Then, that evening, as I was beginning to prepare dinner in the galley, the crew decided to make some serious sail adjustments. The result was a significant change in the boat's movement, making my task below doubly difficult. "Why do we go for hours without altering the boat's motion, and then, just as I begin my balancing act in the galley, you guys decide to make changes? You could either warn me, or wait till I am done down here," I snapped as I gathered food off the cabin floor.

While it was true that the boat could handle the sea better than the crew, I thought I could withstand anything simply by turning it off in my mind. But the reality of dirt, water, constant and erratic motion, shifting goods, and no apparent progress toward our destination, finally had chipped away at my most powerful resolve. I needed a dramatic change if I was to keep it together for the next few days.

If we had remembered that the previous day was a holiday in Canada we would have asked the skipper to give us the day off. But there was little celebration on *RABASKA* on Canada Day as we bandaged our raw nerve endings and quietly went about our duties.

I had two black watches that night. The full moon appeared briefly and my thoughts turned to Maureen back in Toronto. Nothing much had changed. The sea was still angry and we were constantly taking water off the port bow. I tried to sleep prior to the watches but it was impossible. Finally, I dozed off for what seemed like a few minutes when I was awakened to go on deck. I had the most difficult time to stay awake during those two watches. To fight off sleep I tightly secured my poncho type headgear so that it covered my mouth and nose, leaving only my eyes open to the weather. I stood facing forward, my back to the compass, and clung to the edge of the dodger. The view of the ocean was magnificent. The bow ascended into the air and then crashed through the waves, flinging water to port and starboard. Every third or fourth wave would cascade over the coach-house roof and vaporize on my face mask if I was unable to duck on time. It felt cold, but refreshing, but when I miscalculated the water oozed through the tiny slit for my eyes. The interplay between the waves and myself kept me awake and alert, as I tried to assess the proper time to duck behind the dodger.

At the same time, I discovered a good way to get exercise. Every now and then, I would turn my back to the dodger and cling to the compass rail. In that position, I was able to do leg exercises, up and down. If the odd wave burst over my back, it failed to penetrate my waterproof suit. After all the sitting and clinging it felt good to get the legs in motion. I wished I had thought of that earlier in the trip. The upper body got plenty of exercise, holding on, pulling lines, working around the boat. But almost everything we did was in a sitting position to protect us from a fall. Having a way to exercise the legs made me feel much better.

When Henk relieved me from my first watch at midnight, I went below. Again, it made no sense to un-*house* myself from the survival suit. I would only have to struggle into it again in four hours time. It was totally wet on the outside, but because the bunks were already soaked,

I figured I could do no further damage. Although the water was again dripping from the lamp fixture, I was sound asleep in a few minutes.

SHORTLY AFTER 0400 I heard a commotion on the deck. It was not time for me for the watch but, since I was sleeping in my *house,* I was able to move quickly to the cockpit. There was a ship coming up on us from the stern. It was still a good distance away, but Peter who was on watch had difficulty recognizing the color of the lights. I was able to identify the green light and told Peter that the ship was a couple of miles to our port and would pass us in that position. But I could see Peter was still worried and the ship was moving very fast through the water. Neither of us wanted to make a mistake.

Henk heard our discussion and came on deck, verifying the ship's position. He immediately went below and attempted to contact it by radio. There was no reply. Meantime on deck we spotted another light in the distance. There were suddenly a number of ships around us. Because of the darkness and the huge waves, it was difficult to say with absolute certainty the direction in which they were traveling. The first ship became very visible, and clearly, we had plenty of sea room. But another ship seemed to be coming very close and Henk suggested we could consider tacking to allow plenty of passing room. After some discussion, we decided to hold our course and it soon became apparent that this was the correct decision.

The second ship, also on our port, passed on the far side of the first one. If we had tacked to the port, we would have been in his direct path. It became obvious to us that the ships were more concerned with each other, than they were with the tiny blip that was *RABASKA*.

As soon as the second ship cleared the first, it suddenly turned and moved in our direction. His red light and the whole superstructure were very visible. We were not sure whether he was changing course because he had passed the other ship or whether he was taking a look at us. He steamed very close to our stern and then hovered there for some time. Again, the skipper attempted to raise him on the radio. Did the ship think we were in need of some kind of assistance? Was he in awe that such a small boat would be out in such severe weather? We had not given any indication that we required assistance unless he was interpreting our radio message as a call for help. Suddenly the ship sped up and disappeared over our starboard quarter.

WHEN YOU READ ABOUT identifying the movement of ships by their lights at night, the descriptions are quite straight forward. When it is dark and stormy, the light very bad, and the seas running high, and the crew exhausted, it is a very difficult task. Adding to this the speed at which the ships were moving and the slow pace that we were sailing, there was not a lot of time to make a solid judgment. Yet such conclusions are critical to survival. Needless to say, this little encounter provided all of us with a few minutes of excitement. When it was over Peter and Henk went below and I was left alone to continue the watch. The change from excitement to routine was sudden and emotionally draining.

At the end of the watch, I again went below and slept in my wet survival suit. It was a fitful sleep as I was restless and anxious to finish off this leg of the journey. We needed something desperately to lift our spirits. I decided the crew needed a good breakfast. Now at sea a good breakfast is a relative term. In the morning in spite of the roll of the boat, I managed to cook luncheon meat, fried eggs, bread, jam, cheese and plenty of hot coffee.

As we were finishing breakfast, yet another ship appeared on the horizon. It was a huge tanker, and he literally sped past us on the starboard side. His bow wave was huge and the sea was breaking over his port quarter. I have seen ships plowing through the waves with the water coming up over the bow and crashing down on their decks. This was the first time I had ever seen a ship where the waves were crashing over its sides causing all but the pilothouse to disappear under water. No wonder they were breaking over our tiny vessel.

The more frequent appearance of ships indicated that we were closing the gap and getting closer to Gibraltar. That meant rather than scanning the horizon every twenty minutes, the watch had to be more alert and do a complete scan about every ten minutes. It also pointed out the need to keep the VHF radio on at all times.

We spotted four more ships during the afternoon. By sundown, the wind once more began to increase, reaching 30 to 35 knots. Would it ever leave us alone?

I was again on deck for the midnight shift. It was still impossible to sleep during my time below. We were all restless and everyone seemed to have lost their appetite. My only blessing was that my lower back was much better. I had to be careful not to bump it again as I moved about the boat.

The sky was clear and the moon was there to lift my spirits. The stars were so beautiful when they were open to our view. I was angry with myself for not knowing more about them. During the watch I saw our first fishing boat, identifiable by its bright working lights—another sign that the shore was not too distant. We were only three hundred miles out, but unlike the American side of the ocean, there were very few fishing boats. Perhaps we saw so many on the other side because of our proximity to the Grand Banks. There were no other signs of life here however—no birds, dolphins, turtles, flying fish or even whales.

During Henk's watch, I went below and collapsed into the quarter berth. I had not slept in the quarter berth before, but Peter was asleep in the relatively dry berth on the starboard side. The water was literally running down the inside of the boat and the berth was drenched. Again, I did not bother to take off my survival suit. I found the space short and narrow and impossible to dodge the drips and running water. I could not stretch out. The heel of the boat kept pushing me up against the weeping bulkhead. I don't know how Henk slept there. I lay awake hoping Peter would soon replace the skipper on deck so that I could grab his bunk during the exchange of watch.

Unfortunately, Henk stayed beyond the end of his watch giving Peter a chance to get some much needed sleep. When Peter finally got up, I lunged out of the quarter berth and into the one he had just vacated. It was not much dryer, but it was longer and wider and Peter's body had kept it warm.

I was keeping my *house* on below deck more and more, not only because it was the only way to stay dry, but also because the effort to change in and out of it exhausted me. Usually I kept the suit hanging on the inside handrail in the main salon on the port side of the boat. I used a small line to tie it up so that it would hang and air as much as possible. A few times, I was awakened in the night when the suit was swinging back and forth with the motion of the boat, reaching out and touching me. It resembled a dancer in the shadows of the cabin, serenading us with its provocative motions.

Chapter 26

Early the next morning we noticed a tear in the jib and it was necessary to go on deck and lower it for repairs. One of the extra halyards had wrapped around the reefed portion of the jib, and we had a desperate struggle to clear the lines and get the jib safely down on deck.

During this exercise, a huge cargo vessel slowly came close to us and then stopped. They seemed to be observing our actions and assessing our need for assistance. When we had replaced the sail and got underway once again, the huge ship moved off. We tried calling him on the radio to express our thanks, but as usual, we got no answer.

Shortly after this effort, we began to notice that the wind was finally lifting, finally giving us a smoother ride. We decided to set the mainsail as well. We had not shaken out the reef since leaving Ponta Delgada so it was only a matter of releasing it off the boom and pulling it up the mast. It looked like a simple job, and because I was below and not dressed in my wet gear at the time, the skipper went on deck alone. In the process, he lost the winch handle over the side. It is always serious to lose gear overboard, but it is easier on the crew when it's the skipper who was responsible for the error. It was also just another setback for Henk who had spent so much money, planned for so long and worked so hard to make the trip one to remember. His only comment was, "I will never, never cross the Atlantic Ocean again except in a 747 as a passenger. That's all, and you can quote me." I have done so a few times since!

During the afternoon, all three of us huddled under the dodger, trying to soak up the warmth of the sun and lift our spirits. We discussed how much longer to the Gib and we all agreed that it could not be more than two days away. Later we had a nice supper under the dodger, all three of us squeezed together out of the wind and spray. We even had fruit and cookies for dessert.

I went below to read for a while and was informed that I had drawn the watch at 0200. This pleased me, as it meant I could get a good long sleep before having to return to the deck. I was just settled when Peter called me back on deck to give him a hand with the jib lines. As had become our custom we had taken down the main after supper. Because the wind was picking up, Peter wanted to reduce the jib even further before dark. When he went to roll in the sail, both sheets, even though they had double stop knots in the end, blew right through the blocks and were flying in the wind off the side of the boat. He had to go on deck to retrieve them, and needed someone, not only to assist, but as a safety precaution.

Thinking this would be a quick maneuver, I simply jumped out into the cockpit without putting on my safety harness or tether, Peter went forward, grabbed the starboard sheet, worked out the knot, brought it along the lower deck and got it through the block next to me. My job was to tie the stop knot in the end after feeding it through the block. But just then the boat did a sudden lurch. I lost my balance and was projected to the starboard side. I reached up to grab the safety line, but missed, and my upper body went under the line, heading for the water that was rushing by the side of the boat. At the last instant, I released the jib sheet and made a grab for the teak rail. Fortunately I caught it and was able to prevent the rest of my body from being thrown into the dark sea.

Because Peter was engaged on deck under very tough conditions, and Henk was off watch below trying to sleep, I doubt if either one would have realized I had gone overboard. Given the lateness in the day and the high winds and waves, the chances of them finding me would have been close to zero. No one was available to punch the Man Overboard button on the GPS. It was turned off to conserve power anyway!

In my haste to help Peter and return to the cabin, I had broken our cardinal rule. I had been careless about my safety harness. It could have cost me my life. It only takes a few seconds for something catastrophic to happen and even though Peter needed help immediately, I should have taken the time to prepare myself properly and to hold on with one hand. We had resolved never to go on deck without the safety line, and I was just too tired to make the effort. When the task was completed, I went below and climbed into my survival suit before lying down to meditate on what had just almost happened to me. One careless mistake can cost a life in an instant. Fatigue is a deadly enemy on the high seas.

WHEN I LATER CAME on deck for my watch, we were in the midst of another storm. With only two days to go, the North Atlantic still wanted to punish us. It did not give up. The barometer had been falling rapidly during the day, the winds were at Force #8, and the waves were climbing back to twelve feet. To make matters worse, we were now in the direct shipping lane to Gibraltar. In these circumstances, we could not abandon the deck watch and go below and wait out the storm. It was far too dangerous. So all three of us were on deck, looking in every direction, huddled, tired and cold, under the dodger. Around 0300 Peter suggested that Henk and I go below and try to get some sleep. But we were back on deck again an hour later and Peter looked like a drowned rat. His Mother Teresa cowl was plastered to his head, and his gray beard was dripping water onto his soaked jacket.

AROUND 0800 THE WIND began to abate, the barometer started to rise again, and the morning sun came through the clouds. But the spray continued to pour over the boat and keep everything wet. *RABASKA* was living up to its reputation as a wet boat.

We sat together discussing the night's adventures when someone yelled, "There is a ship!!!" None of us had been looking. After a long and exhausting night, we were feeling too sorry for ourselves, and this huge ship came steaming out the rising sun. It was difficult to see and we did not spot it until it was almost on top of us. Although it was only a few hundred yards away, it was the closest call of the voyage. Again, luck was on our side. We did not see him and we could only presume that he saw us.

We were restless, not only because of the most recent storm, and the fact there were more freighters appearing around us, but because we knew we were somewhere between the coast of Portugal and North Africa. We were too far offshore to see land, but just knowing it was out there was a great consolation. If we were to have a serious accident, rescue was within striking distance. The talk was all, "When I get to Gibraltar I am going to…"

Chapter 27

Bᴇᴄᴀᴜsᴇ ᴛʜᴇ sᴜɴ ʜᴀᴅ been out most of that day, and because the shipping was increasing, our spirits were slowly lifting. It was possible in the late afternoon to again sit under the dodger and enjoy the warmth. We also kept the companionway open so the sun could filter down into the cabin and provide the illusion that it was a pleasant and cozy place.

I decided to venture up on the foredeck as the spray coming over the bow seemed to be less frequent and limited to the port side of the boat. This was my first opportunity since leaving Toronto to stretch on the deck in the sunshine. As I sat on the side of the coach-house roof, my legs dangling down on the low side of the boat, I realized the cabin roof was dry. I removed my wet clothes, all of them, and hung them on the starboard safety line. It was such a great feeling to expose my body to the sun's rays, and to think that I was finally going to get my bottom dry. I lay on my stomach to allow the sun to caress my crinkled posterior.

After about forty-five minutes, and with only a couple of small waves sliding down the lower deck, I felt dry. My clothes were warm and well-aired. I slipped into my shorts, gathered up the rest of my clothing from the rail, and started to move into the cockpit. As I stepped around the dodger, the waves could not let me get away with the luxury of dry underwear. One huge wave came over the front, down the side of the boat and whacked me in the rear end. My few minutes of warmth had come to a very sudden and wet end. No pun intended.

During this period we had opened the hatches and portholes as well in order to air the cabin. But the cushions were so wet and drizzled with salt that they would have to be pulled apart and washed with fresh water. The same thing could be said of our clothes and sleeping bags. I suspected the bags would not be recoverable as they were beginning to show signs of rot.

Toward evening, the barometer appeared to be dropping yet again and even though we were now only seventy miles from Tangier, we could still be faced with yet another storm.

Given the length of our voyage and the need to keep records, it was absolutely necessary to do accurate calculations daily. Keeping track of the barometer was one of the best predictors of future weather. In general, if the marker arm, called a hand, is lower than 1000-1004 millibars the weather is being influenced by a low-pressure system. If the arm reads above 1020 mb there will probably be a high-pressure system. The higher or lower the hand, the more extreme the influence of the coming weather. More importantly, the more rapid the change, the worse the weather and the wind. If we saw, for example, that the barometer had changed a few millibars we could go back to our records, and see what the weather was like at a similar reading. With that information, we knew what to expect. More than any other instrument, after the GPS, the barometer was the most valuable tool on-board.

When we were heading into our last night at sea, I decided to have a little fun with Peter, whose responsibility it was to record the barometer readings every day. Each time I went below, I moved the barometer arm down to one that marked an old location. This gave the impression that the barometer was indeed falling rapidly and the weather would deteriorate.

Henk knew I was doing this and when I would call Peter below for another look, Henk would have a great time on deck laughing at what was going on.

Thinking we were in another low, Peter decided to turn in early to get plenty of sleep before the on-coming *storm*. He carefully laid out all of his clothes, being attentive to see that his Mother Teresa cowl was drying on a handrail in the cabin. Then he climbed into a berth and went to sleep. Because of the shipping lanes, we had decided to go with two crew on deck during the night watches.

At 1030 Peter appeared on deck in his full wet gear wondering what happened to the storm. It was a balmy and dry night, and the stars formed a canopy of sparkling light over our heads. This was the sky we had hoped to see frequently during our crossing. When it was my turn to go below, the skipper convinced me that I would be disappointed if

I did not take the chance to enjoy this long awaited pleasure. I agreed and stayed on deck. I got out the book on stars and we tried to identify as many as possible over the next two hours. It was our best night yet, and even though we were not in sight of land or any lights, the smell of the land was in the air.

By 0315 the shipping traffic became constant. By dawn, we had never seen so many ships. There were ships heading into the Strait of Gibraltar and ships steaming out. Where we had encountered so many ships a few nights before, we realized that it was their offshore turning point, some going north, others south and the rest across the ocean. Now, as the water began to narrow, the number of ships increased.

Although I really did not need to get into my survival suit, I did anyway. I had worn it every night for the journey, and I was not going to be without it on our last night at sea.

As DAWN BROKE TRAFFIC was something to behold. On our starboard side, the inbound lane, there was just one ship after another. The same was true on our port side, as ships came out from the Mediterranean and the Suez Canal: tankers, container ships, cargo carriers, war ships and fishing boats of all shapes and sizes. I had never seen so many in one place at the same time. The radio was humming with voices, all in English, as they asked each other for sea room, or made arrangements to put into some port along the way. We were slowly sailing down the middle of this wonderful parade.

Suddenly out of the mists on our starboard side, the hills of Africa slowly emerged. This was my first look at this strange and wonderful continent, and as we drew closer, the city of Tangier, with its red and white buildings, appeared from behind a point of land. We had never been so high in spirits, not only because we were close to port, but also because we were in the middle of such a fleet of ships. With the coast of Africa emerging from the mists, all our previous sufferings suddenly were of no consequence. But there was still no sign of the Rock.

We decided we had to move across the line of outgoing ships in order to get closer to the shore of Spain. The coast of Africa and the coast of Spain would cause our channel to narrow and make it much more difficult to cut through the stream of ships. We altered course and headed for Isla de Tarifa. It was easy to identify by its strange lighthouse, and we heard a radio notice that a fleet of fishing boats was leaving the harbor. We could see the small vessels coming out into the bay and knew exactly where we were.

As we edged through the out coming vessels, we noticed another sailboat about five miles behind us. Suddenly we heard Jacob on the radio calling us. He did not know it was *RABASKA* he was calling because we were too far apart for precise identity. When Peter answered the radio, Jacob could not believe that we were ahead of them.

Along the coast of Spain, there were thousands of modern windmills to generate electricity. I was surprised how barren and bleak the hills were. They looked like rows of freshly baked bread. After the lush islands of the Azores, those hills appeared almost desert-like.

The wind was very light and a slight easterly surface current carried us toward the Mediterranean Sea. The surface current flows into the Mediterranean, but over two hundred feet below there is a sub current rushing into the Atlantic Ocean. We approached the Gut, the bottleneck between the Pillars of Hercules, the gateway to the Mediterranean Sea.

We were fascinated by the huge number of ships and the constant chatter on the radio. One ship called us and asked us to move a little closer to the shore. Our skipper was worried about some ships that seemed to be out of the traffic stream. In the constricted water between the outgoing traffic and the shore, there were some slower ships moving through the narrows. We found ourselves between the shore and this steady stream of ships heading to sea.

Straight ahead of us, the Rock abruptly emerged from the mist and seemed to rise out of the sea. In spite of all the activity, we were in a very unusual place. The Rock is 1,398 feet of limestone and it is easily recognized without the aid of a chart. The Romans considered the Rock to be the end of the world because they believed there was nothing beyond. For the early Greeks it was one-half of the Pillars of Hercules, the other half being on the North African side. For them it marked the end of the civilized world. No wonder the ancients were impressed. It was not only the announcement that the end of our journey was in sight, but its presence and history made it an exciting landfall for three very tired sailors.

Although we did not need a guidebook to identify Gibraltar, we did need a chart to see where the harbor was located. When we were about eight miles from port, the wind decided to take one last kick at us. Suddenly out of the west, a howling wind of over 35 knots struck the boat. The wind is called the Levanter. I had experienced this same type of sudden wind, the Meltemi, a few years previously while cruising in the Greek Islands. It is peculiar to the Mediterranean and has many names depending on where you are, such as La Bora, le Mistral or the Sirocco.

Because it was early dawn, we had not put up the mainsail. All we had to do for the last time was to reef the jib. We were not exactly sure where the harbor was located, and coming in at that speed made it even more difficult to locate.

As we approached Gibraltar Bay, the lighthouse on Europa Point became very visible. We needed to keep the light to starboard and sail along the west side of the island. Gibraltar Harbor is situated on the north end near the runway for the airport. The south and north moles, the long breakwaters protecting Gibraltar Harbour, had to be bypassed in order to reach the Customs Dock which was located between the runway and the Europort.

We saw some small sailboats at the north end of the Rock and we headed in that direction, sailing through a number of large cargo vessels anchored in the Europort. Finally, we saw the opening in the wall and the control tower for the airport, a navigation aid, so we dropped the sail and motored to the Customs and Immigration Dock.

After clearing customs, we radioed the marina across the harbor and arranged for a dock. We moved over quickly, tied up the boat, and all three of us ran for the hot shower. Once refreshed, we then phoned Toronto to let our wives know we were safely docked. Maureen's voice sounded so good I wanted to go home right then and there.

Jacob arrived on the dock and said his skipper was quite surprised that we had come across from the Azores so quickly. It appeared that they had pushed the boat under full sail and the strong winds blew them down the coast of Africa. Hence, they had to beat up to Gibraltar, which took two extra days. Jacob was not happy during the last part of the voyage and told us that even though he had joined them for the full journey from Florida to Israel, he was going to leave the boat in Gibraltar and fly home. We invited him to join us for dinner that evening after which we returned to the boat for a peaceful and full night's sleep.

Chapter 28

I COULD NOT BELIEVE THAT I woke up at 0500. The sunrise over the Rock was magnificent.

This alone made it worth being up so early. After breakfast, we walked uptown through the old walls of the city, and because it was Saturday, the streets were packed with tourists. Gibraltar is a tax free (VAT) city, and attracts thousands of shoppers from nearby Spain. About 34,000 people live on these 2.5 square miles of land. For the past three hundred years, it has been an English colony and the citizens are not interested in having the land returned to Spain. Indeed, Spain closed the border for sixteen years, even cutting off the mail and phone lines. The city is completely bi-lingual and there are some residents who talk about political independence for the Rock.

Unlike the farms of the Azores, there was little sign of cultivation and seemingly no manufacturing. What did all these people do for a living? We learned that, back in the 60s, they wanted to make it into a banking and financial center and to develop tourism. They built Europort, the marinas and waterside condominiums. But these facilities seemed to be languishing for the business never arrived. Most tourists come and shop for a day and then leave. During our first walkabout, we were on the lookout for travel agencies for Peter and Jacob to arrange flights home. There was only one carrier in and out of Gibraltar so reservations to London were a must. Peter wanted to stay and help with cleaning the boat but he had to get back to work as soon as possible. Henk and I planned to sail the boat up the Spanish coast where Henk had made arrangements to winter *RABASKA* for the next leg of the journey.

That evening the skipper treated all of us to dinner at a restaurant near the marina. On the way back on the long pier that led out to the finger docks, Peter was singing in full voice. Again, the songs were in German and it was obvious he was having a good time. It was a great feeling, but sad as well, for it meant Peter would be leaving us soon. I tried to stay a few steps in front of them and said to everyone that passed by, "I am not with that group."

Now that we were in port, Henk had moved back into the V-berth and Peter had settled down in the quarter berth. I stayed with the pullout berth on the starboard side, as the larger berth to port was still wet in spite of our efforts to wash and dry the cushions.

Together, and with Jacob as part of our group, we explored the fascinating history of Gibraltar. We did the tour of the mountain, visited the graveyards and tunnels, and enjoyed the view from the top of the Rock. From there we could see seventeen miles across the water and could make out the Moroccan coast and the Jabal Musa, the Pillars of Hercules, on the other side. Besides the Barbary apes, or tailless monkeys that are fed by the local tourist company, Gorham's Cave, with its history of 100,000 years was the most interesting feature of the mountain.

WE HAD LONG DISCUSSIONS as to what to do with the boat. Because of the leaking, it did not make sense to carry on with our journey into the Mediterranean. Maureen had already decided not to meet us, and the bad weather, along with the Levanter, led to our decision to look into the possibility of shipping *RABASKA* back to Halifax, and from there to Toronto by truck for repairs.

The night before we walked Peter and Jacob to the airport, we again had dinner together and Jacob presented each of us with a beautiful penlight. Since then Jacob has visited us in Toronto and we have cruised together on Henk's new boat.

I had promised Henk that I would stay with him in Gibraltar till the situation was resolved. After the others were gone we explored a number of alternatives regarding the future of *RABASKA*. Selling it in Gibraltar was out of the question. All the boats coming into the marina were either finishing a cruise on the Mediterranean, or having crossed the Atlantic, were ending their trip and flying home. As a result, there were many boats for sale and very few buyers. Some of them looked as if they had been there for months.

Finally, we arranged with a small company to look after the boat and we spoke to a shipping firm and asked for an estimate on the cost to ship the boat home in a container from La Linea, Spain. When Henk had this business finished to his satisfaction, we purchased our air tickets and began the process of dismasting the boat and getting it ready for its trip back to Toronto.

The morning after Peter's serenade on the dock, he crawled out of the quarter berth, turned to me and said, "It ain't over, till it's over, and the fat lady sang on the dock last night."

RABASKA SAT QUIETLY AT dock in Gibraltar. The cost of shipping it home from there was prohibitive. The skipper arranged to have repairs made over the winter and then he returned, the next summer with a new crew to sail the boat back to Toronto.

As for me it still ain't over nor will it ever be over even if the fat lady sang that night on the dock for Peter. This journey changed who I am. It taught me the fragility of life, my need to depend on and trust others and it opened my eyes to the daily miracles of sunsets, color, friends and most of all, my love for Maureen. Thank you Henk and Peter.

Dick Grannan